High Risk, High Reward

The Journey of an "Underdog Entrepreneur"
Who Took Chances, Overcame Obstacles,
and Built a $50 Million Business

Steve Scher

High Risk, High Reward: The Journey of an "Underdog Entrepreneur"
Who Took Chances, Overcame Obstacles, and Built a $50 Million Business

This book is for informational purposes only. It does not provide specific business or legal advice and should not be relied on as such. The author does not guarantee that the information in this book is accurate, complete, up to date, or will produce certain financial results. The material is general in nature and cannot substitute for professional advice. All trade names and product names are property of their respective owners. Further, the author is not liable if the reader relied on the material and was financially damaged in some way. Any statements about the recollection of stories shared are recalled to the best of the author's knowledge.

Printed in the United States of America

Library of Congress Cataloging-in-Publication Data
Scher, Steve
High Risk, High Reward:
The Journey of an "Underdog Entrepreneur" Who Took Chances,
Overcame Obstacles, and Built a $50 Million Business / by Steve Scher.
ISBN: 978-1-7334485-0-5
Library of Congress Control Number: 2019915497

Cover and book design: Karen Saunders
Editor: Patrice Rhoades-Baum

Steve Scher
Chief Executive Officer
Small Business Advisor | Speaker
Acrobat Advisors, LLC
Steve@AcrobatAdvisors.com
www.AcrobatAdvisors.com

Dedication

I would like to dedicate this book to my immediate family members and my Acrobat "family." This book would not have happened without your help and support.

Acknowledgements

I would like to thank my "Dream Team" (Karen, Mary, Melinda, and Patrice) for making this book possible. Without your guidance, dedication and commitment, sharing this story would not be possible.

Table of contents

The greatest challenge and the greatest reward

The entrepreneurial spirit is often motivated by money, independence, and lifelong dreams. I knew early on that I was meant to be an entrepreneur. I wanted to live the dream of owning my own business. I wanted to control my own destiny. I spent the early part of my career learning about business by working for other companies – making mistakes and learning from them, learning how to lead people, and learning how to run a company efficiently. But I always knew that one day I'd do my own thing. What I didn't realize about owning my own business was the effect that entrepreneurs can have on other people.

When I first decided to write this book, I wanted to share my real-life experiences through the entire lifecycle of a business. What started out as a dream grew into a leading temporary staffing company with offices around the country that ultimately sold for millions. And let me tell you, being a business owner was the hardest thing I've ever done. In this book, I want to provide an inside look at how I got there and the obstacles I had to overcome in order to achieve that success. The entrepreneurial journey is rewarding, but it's also filled with so many unexpected twists and turns.

If you're lucky, you have a mentor to run ideas past, someone who can give you seasoned advice. But for most of us, it can be lonely at the top. As I built my company, I wanted an objective, expert opinion to help me process major business decisions and help me grow my business. I could not go to my employees, because it was my responsibility to run the business as I saw fit. I relied on business books for sage advice and, frankly, on my gut instinct.

As the business owner, you're responsible for the business and all the decisions you make. Sometimes as an entrepreneur or business owner you feel as though you're on an island by yourself, relying on your gut instinct for all of your decisions. That's exactly what I did. By sharing my story, I want to help other business owners and aspiring entrepreneurs.

The more I thought back on those years and what I'd really learned from my experiences, the more I realized that the greatest reward of entrepreneurship is what you can do for others.

When I bought my company, I thought it would be a good way to make a living. I quickly learned that the opportunities I gave others would be so much more rewarding than any amount of money. Employees come from all walks of life. They are all motivated by different things. Some of your employees will be motivated by money, others will be motivated by responsibility, and others will be motivated by positive reinforcement. That said, giving people careers is a huge responsibility. I know I needed to provide my people a work environment that enabled them to achieve success. My employees counted on me for their paycheck as well as their career path and their personal and professional growth. They relied on me to make the right decisions about my business, so they would have job security. I did not take this responsibility lightly.

I realized that the success of any business starts with the people you surround yourself with. But more important, your employees are an integral part of that success. It's an entrepreneur's responsibility to provide employees with all the tools necessary to be successful. An entrepreneur needs to be as transparent as possible and be able to empower his or her employees to make sound business decisions. And if you can get your employees to buy into your vision and reward them for the success of that business, then you're onto something big.

The entrepreneurial journey is the ultimate challenge. It's hard work every day. My goal for this book is to provide insight into the struggle and inspire you to go for it anyway. If you're in the throes of running your own business, I hope this book will inspire you to keep forging ahead – while providing insight into creative solutions that can lead to success.

To that end, I've included multiple "On-Target Business Advice" sections in this book to share hard-won business lessons. These bonus sections offer additional details on a focused topic. My hope is that you'll return to this book again and again to take advantage of this advice and insight. Topics include:

- Low risk, low reward/High risk, high reward: My recipe for success

- How to strategically hire military veterans, reformed ex-offenders, and people with special needs

- How to make technology work for you and your bottom line

- Real-world tips to create a culture of agility and loyalty

- Growing your business: Acquisition versus organic growth

- Tips to build out your business to maximize the value

- How to conduct extensive due diligence prior to acquiring a company

- Checklist to prepare your exit strategy, so you can get the highest sale price possible

Introduction

The entrepreneurial journey can offer the greatest challenge and the greatest reward. This is my story.

Chapter 1

Taking the biggest risk of my life

Early in my career, I was national sales manager for an Internet company that provided high-speed Internet to hotels. Back then, if you wanted to get online at a hotel, you had to pull out the phone plug and plug your computer line into the wall jack. Then you had to cross your fingers and hope for access. This company was first to provide high-speed Internet exclusively to the hospitality industry. This service was way ahead of its time. The thought of hotels converting their properties to high-speed Internet was still in its infancy. Therefore, the first couple of years I worked for this Internet company, all I did was prospect. I was selling the future of what high-speed Internet could look like to the hospitality industry – how it could create new income streams and differentiate a given hotel from other hotels that didn't offer this service.

What really fascinated me about my time at this company was the fact that the founder had a vision and took a big risk. This entrepreneur had the foresight and belief that one day all hotels would have high-speed Internet. And boy was he right. It didn't take long before the phones were ringing off the hook. High-speed Internet became a must-have service throughout the entire hospitality industry, and we were first to market.

That's when I realized it was time for me to embark on the journey of entrepreneurship. I wanted to create a must-have product or service. But what would it be? Would I have to buy an existing business or create a business of my own? The wheels in my brain started to turn. I wanted to control my own destiny.

I've always had an entrepreneurial spirit. I grew up in a working-class family; my father hung draperies for a living, and my mom was a stay-at-home mother. We didn't have a lot of money. Our big vacation every year was in February when we'd drive from New Jersey to Florida to visit my grandparents. We'd stop at Disney World, but we never stayed at Disney World. We'd stay at the Days Inn for two or three days. We were happy, but money was tight.

I remember on one trip to Florida we stopped for pizza, and this amazing idea struck me: Eating pizza would be so much easier if it were cut into bite-size pieces! I spent the entire trip figuring out how I could create pizza bites and fantasizing about the business I'd build. I drew sketches and everything. As soon as we got to Florida, I told my grandfather all about it. Frozen food companies eventually had the same great idea. This was a passing childhood fantasy, but I remember how much fun it was, imagining what my own business would look like.

Those trips to Florida spawned other entrepreneurial efforts. I used to buy fireworks in South Carolina and sell them to the kids in New Jersey, because you couldn't get fireworks there. That business didn't last very long, because one of the kids threw smoke bombs in the hallway at our junior high school, and I got into a lot of trouble for it. When I got a little older, I helped my cousin wash floors in bungalows where we used to spend our summers. I liked the freedom of not punching anyone's time clock.

Years later, when I started feeling like I'd done all I could do in my sales job, following that entrepreneurial spirit and owning my own business was the only thing on my mind.

While I was still working at the Internet company, I had an idea to start a haircutting salon for men and boys. I wanted to create a haircutting experience as opposed to just opening another barber shop. It would be a place where fathers could take their kids for haircuts, and it would feel like walking into a sports bar where you'd be surrounded by televisions and video games. I had it all figured out; this would be my thing. I was going to call it At The Buzzer. I was determined to get this business concept off the ground and finally be able to live the American dream by owning my own business.

However, I realized there two big obstacles. First, while I was sitting in the parking lot of a strip mall in front of Great Clips, I realized I wouldn't be able to make much money in this type of business. I'd have to cut hair for sixty people every day just to pay the rent. The second obstacle was the fact that my original concept had already been rolled out to the marketplace. It was called Sport Clips. So that was the end of At The Buzzer. But if you believe in yourself, you are committed, you have an exciting concept, and the time is right, don't let anything get in the way of starting your own business.

I was aching to do my own thing and had cultivated a relationship with a business broker. I'd been working with him for about six months when he told me about a tiny temporary staffing company being sold on the QT. He said, "Steve, I've known you for about six months. I've listened to you and learned what your needs are. I know your strengths and weaknesses, and I think I've found a company that would be a good fit for what you're looking for. The owner is interviewing potential buyers next week."

I was lukewarm about the idea, because I never imagined myself in the temporary staffing industry, and I didn't know anything about it. I was a technology and hospitality guy. But as I processed this potential business opportunity, I started connecting with the idea. I did some soul searching, and the more I thought about it, the more I liked the idea. This small company had a lot of potential. In addition, the business model played to my professional strengths.

They say nothing teaches you more about yourself than owning your own business. I would tell every entrepreneur to think about his or her strengths when considering an opportunity. Even in the early days, I knew my own strengths and weaknesses.

When you look at doing your own thing, play to your strengths. Work in an industry that's a good fit for you. And spend a great deal of time learning about yourself and realistically assessing your strengths and weaknesses.

My biggest strength is my people skills – I love inspiring, leading, and mentoring. Owning a temporary staffing business would let me use those skills.

However, I believe there are two types of people: dreamers and doers. I was always more of a dreamer. I always dreamed about having my own business, but when I was faced with a real opportunity, I was afraid to take the plunge. I had a family that relied on me both financially and emotionally. The thought of walking away from a steady, six-figure salary was almost too much to handle. For me to actually invest my life savings, take the risk, and buy a company would be a huge jump. The opportunity to buy this temporary staffing company sounded good, but I hesitated.

The business broker was a very good negotiator. He persisted. He said, "Steve, I think you owe it to yourself to meet with this owner. It's a long shot anyway, because there are eight other potential buyers interested in this business."

So I met with the owner. He explained the business to me – he had started a small staffing company that provided extra wait staff for hotels and events – and he interviewed me about my experience. During our conversation, we connected because of my background in the hotel business. I went to school for hotel management and spent many years with Hyatt Corporation. He also went to school for hotel management. We had a great conversation and clicked right away. Not long after that meeting, the owner told the business broker he wanted to sell me the business. Acrobat Outsourcing would be mine if I wanted it. He was asking $350,000.

We went through a due diligence period for about six weeks. By this time, I really had the jitters. This was the closest I'd ever gotten to owning my own business, and my bank account balance didn't come close to $350,000. But I hired a bookkeeper, and we went through all his books. The company's annual revenue was $200,000. There were two internal employees and about forty temporary employees. All business was one-off deals; this company didn't have any vendor contracts or large accounts. But still, I saw an opportunity. I thought I could make money. After due diligence, I offered $290,000 with a down payment of twenty percent and the rest on a five-year note. He took it.

After all those years of dreaming about owning a business, you'd think I would've been celebrating this deal. But I remember, even while I was moving forward, being so nervous about it. As soon as we made the verbal agreement, I thought, "What have I done?" I was leaving a job making a quarter of a million dollars a year to chase some dream. And the previous owner had only paid himself $40,000 a year. I felt like a crazy person. My wife at the time was nervous too. She believed in me, but we had just started a family, and she was extremely conservative. Losing my paycheck was a big deal, and she didn't want me to take that plunge.

I second-guessed my decision so much that I called the broker and told him I'd made a mistake. He said, "Steve, you have to go for it."

Something in my gut made me feel that he was right. So I went for it. I signed the papers. Two weeks later I was the proud owner of Acrobat Outsourcing. However, I had no idea what I was really getting myself into.

My first clue came when we went into escrow, and the business location was divulged. The Tenderloin had the highest crime rate of any area in San Francisco. It was easily the roughest area in the city, with more homelessness, prostitution, and drug dealing than anywhere else. And the Acrobat office was right in the middle of where it all took place. Right in the heart of the Tenderloin.

On my first day as owner, I remember parking my car and walking to this office, saying to myself, "What have I done?" I was panhandled and had to step over homeless people to get to the building's door. My new office was located on the second floor above a picture-framing shop, and the ceilings were only six feet high. Anyone over six feet tall would have to bend over. This bad situation got even worse when I walked in the door and introduced myself as the new owner.

The two employees had no idea the business had been for sale. It turned out the company had been run by a semi-absentee owner. He hadn't been working in the business except to send invoices once a week. No one was doing anything to grow the company. Worse, one of the two employees had been under the impression that he would take over the business. The news I delivered that morning, from their perspective, wasn't good. This only deepened my fear that I'd made a huge mistake.

I remember sitting at my desk, looking out the window, watching a drug deal, and feeling more nervous than ever. I just gave up my life savings to own an itty-bitty staffing company with two employees. The woman was covered from head-to-toe in tattoos and, I soon learned, was in and out of jail all the time. The other (Larry) was hostile toward me, because he felt like I'd bought the business out from under him – in the worst location ever! And this was just the first day.

But I had to make it work. I wasn't going to let down my family. If I failed, I'd lose everything. I had to convince my wife I could do this. If I failed, she'd have the permanent right to say, "I told you so." My pride was too big to walk away from this.

In the next few days, the situation only got worse. Larry threatened me and told me that if I wanted him to stay, I'd have to pay him $250,000. So I let him go. I fired the tattooed woman that week too, because she turned out to be totally unreliable, showing up several hours late one day, and not showing up at all the next day. But I was determined, even though I had to build the business from scratch. I wasn't going to fail.

I never knew that being an entrepreneur meant fighting for your business every day. In those first days owning Acrobat, I was immediately put into a position where I had to fight for my business. I was the salesperson, I was the temp employee recruiter, I was the staffing manager, I was the finance manager, and I was the HR manager. I was working sixteen hours a day to get this business off the ground. When I wasn't selling our temp services to hotels, hospitals, and other potential customers, I would come back to the office try to find temp employees to staff the few jobs I could find. When I wasn't selling or staffing, I was invoicing. When I went home, if temp employees called out sick, I continued to make calls to staff positions and fulfill my obligations to my customers. I was taking calls 24/7 just to get this business off the ground. Despite all my effort in those first few weeks, I started losing business.

Companies I had set up with temp employees were calling and cancelling their orders. I couldn't figure out what was happening until a client told me that my ex-employee had started his own staffing company. She said, "Steve, I just had a visit from Larry. He told me you have no idea what you're doing, you have no experience in temp staffing, you don't know the temp employees, and you had the audacity to fire him. Larry said I was in luck, though, because he was starting his own temp staffing company. Just so you know, Larry has your price list and your customer list. I told him I was loyal to Acrobat. But, Steve, if you mess up once, I'm going to take my business to Larry. He offered me a lower price."

As if things weren't bad enough, I had a guy out there actively taking my customers. That's when I realized that I would have to fight hard for my business every day – and that entrepreneurship would be the fight of my life.

On-target business advice

Low risk, low reward/High risk, high reward: My recipe for success

I've learned throughout my personal life and professional career that hard work pays off. You need to put in the time, be open to change, and be committed to your craft (whatever that might look like to you). And most important, be true to yourself. If you follow this advice, chances are you'll live a "satisfied" life.

However, most entrepreneurs I've come across (myself included) aren't content with just a "satisfied" life. They want more. They want financial independence, they want the ability to better other people's lives, they want to call the shots and, ultimately, they want to control their own destiny. Entrepreneurs are risk takers, and I'm no different. I believe the higher the risk, the higher the reward. However, before you make any high-risk decisions, I urge you to do your homework first.

The first thing you need to do is believe in yourself. Take a step back and look at yourself objectively. Have you been successful in your personal and professional life? Have you learned from past mistakes? Do you have the savviness and ability to overcome obstacles? Can you recover both emotionally and financially if the risk you're taking doesn't meet your expectations?

Ready to take a risk?
Ask yourself these questions...

I always ask myself three questions before I make a high-risk decision:

1. Based on my decision, what would be the worst-case scenario?

2. What would be the best-case scenario?

3. What would be the most likely scenario?

If I am at peace with the outcome of each scenario, then most likely I would make the decision to move forward. When buying my company, I stepped through the three questions:

1. What would be the worst-case scenario? I would lose my life savings, be forced to get another job, and need to rebuild my savings account. I was ok with this possible outcome, because I knew I had a lot of experience and could get another job.

2. What would be the best-case scenario? I would thrive at owning my own business, sell it for millions of dollars, and secure a nest egg for retirement. (Luckily, that's how it turned out.)

3. What would be the most likely scenario? I would start my business, struggle early, and continue to chug along. Eventually, I would retire with a steady paycheck. I would be at peace with that decision as well.

Surround yourself with "Builders"

I believe most entrepreneurs are "Architects." They have a vision for what they want their company to look like. They need to surround themselves with "Builders." The Builders are the employees they hire to help them build out their company. While Builders take direction from the owner, these employees usually excel at the entrepreneur's weaknesses. It's vital that entrepreneurs build out a team they can trust and, ultimately, will help build out the company to the owner's expectations. Meanwhile, you are creating a company that your employees are proud to work for — and proud to help build.

Build a great culture

Building culture is one of the entrepreneur's most important responsibilities. It's the vibe of your company. You need to hire talented employees you trust and can count on to help you build out your company – and build a vibrant, productive culture. It's imperative that your employees believe in your vision, and it's important to include them in decisions that help to shape your company.

Keep employees informed about the trials and tribulations of your company. Empower them to make sound business decisions and keep them abreast of the health of your business. Pay a competitive salary and reward your people when they go above and beyond the call of duty. Be creative with their compensation plan. Don't be afraid to pay a commission on new business. If you're making money, then your employees should be making money too.

Be a mentor

You owe it to your employees to help them grow. Take them outside of their comfort zone and ask them to take on additional responsibilities if you see that they're ready for it. Get to know them personally. Learn about their families and hobbies. Take an interest in them. Take your time and push your employees to their limits. Reward them financially and with positive reinforcement. Extra time off goes a long way!

Know your employees' limitations. Don't put your employees into a demanding role if they're not ready for it. Put them in a position where they will succeed. If they cannot keep up with the growth of your business, then let them go. Some companies I consult with have kept employees working there too long. It actually stunted their business growth. Trust me, most employees know when they are big contributors and when they are not. Nine out of ten times, it's a relief to employees when they are let go, because they know they can't keep up with the growth of the business.

Create a work environment where you and your employees are proud to come every day. Select an area that's safe and close to restaurants. Promote work/life balance.

When you launch your business, keep it lean and mean

Be disciplined not to spend money foolishly. Spend money only on must-have items. The nice-to-have items will come in time. However, make sure you dedicate a part of your budget to marketing. It's difficult to measure marketing success but, be rest assured, you need to market your business constantly. Utilize social media. It's free to subscribe to LinkedIn, Facebook, Instagram, and Twitter. Be disciplined to constantly update your social media and engage with your customers and prospects.

It's imperative to work off a budget and forecast

Create a budget to keep track of your expenses and expectations. Create a sales forecast you can use as a roadmap. Make sure both your budget and forecast are realistic and achievable. If not, revise them. You need to follow realistic metrics in order to hit your goals.

Communication is vital to a company

Have weekly or monthly meetings with your employees. Share with them the wins and losses of the company. Keep them apprised of all internal communications. Be careful not to schedule too many meetings — it will affect their productivity. Keep meetings to an hour or less. Evaluate your employees' performance at least once a year. Employees want to know how they're doing. You never want to blindside employees and fire them on performance when they had no idea there was even a performance issue.

Finally, have fun!

Chapter 2

The first big break

As an entrepreneur, you've got to believe in yourself. No matter how bad those early days at Acrobat Outsourcing were, I wasn't going to allow myself to fail. I was extremely frustrated, but I had no choice but to make it work. Thank God I did.

About a month into owning Acrobat, I was driving around, literally trying to save my business by cold calling anyone who might need foodservice staffing. On this particular evening, I was feeling really down about everything. I'd put my life savings into a company that was dying in my arms. I had one small child under the age of three and one on the way. Although I was determined not to fail, I was beginning to wonder if the outcome was out of my hands.

At about 6:00 p.m., I was sitting in my car in the parking lot at one of San Francisco's largest hospitals. I had intended to cold call the foodservice department, but I was feeling so down I practically had tears in my eyes. I was thinking about how I should have stayed in my sales job and thinking I'd made a huge mistake. I was beating myself up, because there were so many challenges about my business that I hadn't realized when I bought it. One issue was the animosity with the employee I'd fired who now was competing against me. There was so much about the situation that I couldn't control. I remember staring at the hospital, coming back to that same question, "What have I done? What have I done?" I was so upset I almost drove home.

But I couldn't go home. Something in me hesitated. If I didn't keep trying, then what was I going to do? Go to my office and feel sorry for myself?

I'd worked in sales for years, and I knew I could cold call. Cold calling can be difficult, but all you really need is a foot in the door and to be likeable. One of my strengths has always been my likability factor. People want to do business with people they like. And I could usually get people to like me. There were a lot of things I couldn't do, but I could cold call. That, and believe in myself.

Plus, I was already there, sitting in the parking lot. I couldn't let myself lose when I knew there was more to do. I got out of the car and went into the hospital. I had a brochure and business card in my hand, and I walked to the front desk and asked for the foodservice department. The receptionist directed me to the basement. I went downstairs, down a dark hallway, and past housekeeping and piles of laundry to the office of Sherry Rodney, the director of nutritional services.

I knocked on the door, but there was no answer. I touched the doorknob, expecting it to be locked. But the door opened. In that split second, I thought I'd leave my brochure on her desk – that would be better than sliding it under the door. But when the door opened all the way, she was sitting at her desk. I said, "Oh, I'm so sorry to bother you. I didn't know you were in the office; I was just going to leave a brochure. My name is Steve Scher, I own a temporary staffing company that specializes in the hospitality and food-service industries. If your cook calls in sick or you need extra staff, you can call me."

Sherry looked at me, baffled, and said, "Wait, what do you do?"

I gave her my sales spiel, explaining that my business provides cooks, dishwashers, servers, bartenders, and cashiers.

"Have a seat," she said. "This might be your lucky day."

"Why's that?" I asked.

"We're bracing for a citywide hospital strike, and I'm going to need 400 employees – cooks, dishwashers, cashiers – and I don't have a resource."

Honestly, sitting there, I don't know if I realized the impact of what she was actually saying.

"The strike is supposed to start in three weeks," she said. "Can you get me 400 employees?"

Ignorance is bliss, and I sure didn't have 400 temporary employees. But I totally put myself out there and said, "Of course I can."

"Great," she said. "You've got three weeks."

In that moment, a month of sleepless nights paid off. Sherry was handing me $2 million in business. Better still, she offered to pay me in advance. If I invoiced her by Wednesday, she'd have the money in my account by Friday, so I could make payroll. This never happens. It was like a gift from God.

But if I walked into that office with big problems, I walked out with what might have been a bigger one. Where would I find 400 temporary employees? In reality, that wouldn't be enough. With attrition and people not showing up, I needed 600 or 700 people. And I had no one to help me find them, because I'd fired my entire staff.

The next day, a solution appeared. Once again, it was like a gift from God. I was sitting in my cramped little office wondering where I could find hundreds of temp employees with no one to help me, when a woman named Rhonda walked in, looking for a job. She knew about Acrobat Outsourcing, because the cafeteria she had worked at used our services. Rhonda was getting ready to move to Chicago and open her own restaurant. She quit her job at the cafeteria but had to wait for her husband to finish a work assignment. She was looking for temporary work for six months.

She was a sharp lady, and I told her immediately that she was hired. But I said, "Rhonda, I'm not going to put you in a temp job. I've got a better job for you. Why don't you help me recruit employees to work this hospital strike? I'll pay you ten percent of the overall revenue of this project."

She agreed to it – thank goodness. So Rhonda and I went to every unemployment office in San Francisco, looking for employees with kitchen experience who'd be willing to cross a picket line and make $9 an hour.

Where do you find people like that? Well, we quickly found out that reformed ex-offenders were ideal employees. People in prison often had to work in the scullery (the prison kitchen). They had the experience, and they were tough enough to cross a picket line! Plus, San Francisco is an extremely liberal city. At that time, the only requirement for foodservice employees was passing a tuberculosis test. So we recruited a lot of reformed ex-offenders through the city's unemployment agencies.

I remember getting a call from the Northern California Service League (NCSL), which rehabilitates ex-offenders. When someone gets out of prison, usually they are placed in transitional housing where they learn about re-entering society while getting their lives back together. Turns out, NCSL was one of the best housing units around. This organization provides its clients with food, clothing, life-skills training, and employment opportunities. It was a one-stop shop for reformed ex-offenders to get back on their feet. This organization became a major recruiting center for qualified temporary employees for Acrobat Outsourcing.

Between NCSL and unemployment agencies, Rhonda and I found several hundred temporary food-service workers in just a few weeks. We brought these employees into my office, conducted an orientation, on-boarded them, and were ready. For three weeks, I never worked so hard in my life.

Most strikes never happen, because the two sides usually work out a deal and agree not to strike. But this strike happened. There were lines of hospital employees with signs and horns and megaphones, tormenting me and my employees when we crossed the picket line. And it was a nasty strike.

I was getting calls from my temp employees that strikers slashed their tires. I was replacing tires. They wrote on the union website that I was a scab. One day, someone threw a smoke bomb into our office! It was scary. I had never experienced anything like this. Week after week, the strike kept going.

Unfortunately, because we were so busy, I found myself spending more time on my strengths than my weaknesses. I spent more time selling the staffing services, staffing the jobs, and taking care of the day-to-day interaction with my temp employees and business customers than I did with the accounting. I wasn't very good at QuickBooks or invoicing. About a month into the strike, I hadn't sent out any invoices. I ran out of capital and thought my business might go under, because I didn't have enough cash to make payroll. Out of desperation, I tapped into my personal home equity line and paid it back as fast as I could. I learned about cash flow the hard way! I had hundreds of temp employees counting on a paycheck. And I stressed about it every week.

I was also dealing with a lot of personal issues at that time. During the first two months that I owned Acrobat, my wife had a miscarriage. And her dad (my father-in-law) passed away at the beginning of the hospital strike. So I was trying to get my business off the ground, managing a huge piece of business with the hospital strike, comforting my wife, and attending a family funeral.

With all the obstacles life throws at you, to be successful you've got to dig deep and juggle and find a way to make it all work. That's what an entrepreneur does. There is no *can't do*. You have to make it work. And I did.

In the middle of the hospital strike ordeal – I was recruiting temp employees, onboarding employees, staffing jobs, and going crazy – a guy named Johnny Diego walked into my office. He was just over five feet tall, Filipino, and a clean-cut guy who stood out in a three-piece suit. He just got out of jail and needed a job. I found a job for him, working as a cafeteria cashier at a large corporation. Johnny worked there about two weeks when he got a call from the cafeteria manager who said they wanted to hire him full-time. This was great news. Johnny gave them his name, Social Security number, and other required information. But when they saw that his crime and prison record was about ten sheets long, they did not give him the job, and they asked me not to send him back.

I felt horrible, because this guy was really trying to get his life back together. Before going to prison, he was a kingpin drug dealer in South San Francisco, making something like $50,000 a week selling crystal meth. When I told him they weren't going to hire him because of his background, Johnny told me the details of his situation. He was trying to get custody of his baby from the mother, because she was on drugs. If he didn't have a job, he couldn't get custody.

As I mentioned, my temporary employees were from all walks of life. This included military veterans, reformed ex-offenders, reformed drug addicts, and people with special needs. Interacting with them, I realized they were looking for someone to believe in them and offer them a second chance. The people who really wanted to work embraced the opportunity. I always believed that when you're young sometimes you make mistakes, but there's no reason to pay for those mistakes for the rest of your life. People deserve second chances, and I believed in Johnny Diego. He was obviously a good worker, and he was motivated. So I hired him to answer phones while he worked out his custody situation.

Well, this guy was so flattered and embraced the job so much that he became my right-hand man. And this was in the very early stages of my company. Because he had been in prison, he knew how to talk to the temp employees who were working during the hospital strike. He also staffed all the other jobs for my other customers.

Johnny was living in a halfway house and absolutely hated it, so he worked really hard and put in long hours. He would come to the office at 6:00 in the morning and work until midnight. I had to kick him out of the office, so he could do something else! Johnny worked every single day. He came in on weekends, so I could take some time off. He did such a great job; he was definitely my savior.

A lot of my temporary employees were just as great. They were used to being paid a nickel an hour in prison, and now they were getting paid more than they ever had in their life. A lot of those employees made the most of this opportunity.

As the strike wore on, I just wanted it to be over. The money was great, but I stopped caring about the money. I wanted my life back.

After nine long weeks, the phone rang in the middle of the night. Initially, I thought there was yet another issue that would need my attention, but this call was different. This was the call I'd been waiting for: the hospital strike was finally over. Both sides agreed on a new contract, and the permanent hospital workers would be back to work the next morning. I remember feeling a great sense of relief, but I also felt conflicted.

Sure, I wanted this strike to be over. Sure, I would miss the money. But what would I do with all of these temp employees who worked so hard for me for the past nine weeks? They relied on me for a job and for a second chance in life – a chance to make an honest living. I was not going to let them down. So I did my best to keep them working. Although I couldn't keep everyone working, because there just weren't enough jobs, I was able to keep many of them working steadily.

I also wanted to show my appreciation to the Northern California Service League, which was so instrumental in helping me find employees. I felt indebted to NCSL and used the strike profits to make a significant donation. This organization became a great strategic partner for my business, and later I became a board member.

Looking back, I learned so much from this experience. There is no doubt the money was great, but the human element was the most eye-opening factor for me. Working with formerly incarcerated people was inspiring. I might not have had the same upbringing as some of the employees who worked for me during the strike, but we all have one thing in common: *We want to be respected regardless of age, ethnicity, and background.* People do deserve a second chance. Most of these folks, given an opportunity, will make the most of that opportunity. Unfortunately, some people just aren't ready yet. But creating opportunities for those who are ready really excited me about what I could do with Acrobat Outsourcing – and how I could impact people's lives.

From that day forward, a new Acrobat was born. The strike generated $1.9 million in revenue. I paid about $900,000 in payroll. I ended up with $1 million in cash. This strike, this opportunity, defined my business in so many ways. It was epic. I put that million dollars right back into the business, which really got us off the ground. Who knows where I'd be today if that strike had never happened? I could still be sitting in that cramped office in the Tenderloin, struggling along.

I believe in God, and I believe in luck. Those months were the hardest I ever worked in my entire career. But perseverance brought that opportunity. And hard work made that opportunity a success.

On-target business advice

How to strategically hire military veterans, reformed ex-offenders, and people with special needs

As a business owner, recruitment can be a challenge, especially in today's economy where unemployment is at a record low and immigration laws are strictly enforced. You need to be as creative as possible to look for ways to recruit employees. Where can you find a resource of available employees? This is a major issue I have come across as I work with other business owners.

My advice is to think outside the box by targeting potential applicants who want to work but sometimes are the ones who are left behind, because many employers are reluctant to hire them. I took the risk of hiring the employees who were left behind, and my risk paid off. Some of these people were the best employees I ever hired.

Military veterans

A great resource for recruitment is targeting military vets. They can make great employees! I found that most military veterans are extremely disciplined, have great work ethic and experience, and tend to be very proud. I recommend contacting your local organizations and introducing yourself as a potential employer for military vets. There are many organizations you can tap into. Here are a few:

- Veterans.gov – This website offers resources from the U.S. Department of Labor for job-seekers and employers who want to hire those who served our country.

- CareerOneStop Veteran and Military Transition Center – This website is a one-stop online shop for employment, training, and financial help for vets after military service.

- Hiring Our Heroes – This is a program of the U.S. Chamber of Commerce Foundation. It's a nationwide initiative to help transitioning service members, veterans, and military spouses find meaningful employment opportunities. The program networks with businesses through the U.S. Chamber of Commerce and it partners with public, private, and nonprofit organizations across the country.

These are just a few of the resources you can tap into; I urge you to contact your local office. Make an appointment, meet face to face with the career counselor, and get a feel for the organization. Once the relationship has been cultivated, start recruiting military veterans to your company. Make sure you interview potential candidates face to face. Ask them pointed questions, look for positive body language, and try to get a feel for their passion and commitment to work. Make sure any disabilities they may have incurred during their service time won't affect their work responsibilities. Conduct a thorough background check.

Reformed ex-offenders

A great resource that tends to be overlooked is hiring reformed ex-offenders. In fact, I call these people Second Chancers. This group is comprised of people from all walks of life. They may have made mistakes in the past, but there comes a point in their lives where they want to make an honest living. They are just looking for companies that are willing to take a chance on them.

Hiring reformed ex-offenders can be challenging but, if done right, they can become a valuable asset to your organization. Ex-offenders are released from either state or federal prisons. The ex-offenders released from state prisons are a bit tricky to hire, because their backgrounds can consist of a variety of crimes, some which can be violent in nature. That's why it's so important to make sure you do a great deal of research on candidates before hiring them. I tell my clients that, before you agree to an interview with candidates, take time to speak to their parole agent first to make sure they're ready to take on this new responsibility.

In addition, most state ex-offenders live in transitional housing or work with nonprofit organizations to help them get back on their feet. Find out which organization they work with and speak to that organization about the individual. Make sure you have a representative of that organization join a face-to-face interview with you or your recruiter. Spend quality time interviewing candidates and trying to get to know them. Ask pointed questions, so you can get a real feel for their commitment to work. Look for eye contact and appearance. Make sure they've received life-skills training and have the tools available to them, so they're ready to re-enter society. Make sure they're determined to make an honest living.

Be very careful who you choose to hire and take time to select the right position for them. You don't want to put someone in a position to fail. For example, if they were convicted of stealing, don't place them in a job that deals with money. Based on my experience, I find that more mature ex-offenders (usually over thirty years old) are done working the streets and are more committed to making an honest living than ex-offenders in their teens or twenties. I find that younger ex-offenders aren't ready to enter society and make an earnest living, because they are so used to hustling on the streets.

The other type of reformed ex-offenders comes from federal prisons. These ex-offenders were convicted of federal crimes such as money laundering, embezzlement, and counterfeiting. Based on my experience, these are highly intelligent folks who, for one reason or another, did something illegal. For the most part, they are professional, have good appearance, and are determined to get back into society and put the past behind them. They can make outstanding employees, because of their intelligence, work ethic, and appearance. However, you need to be careful not to put them in a job where they will have temptation. For example, you don't want to place ex-offenders in jobs taking money if they were convicted of money laundering.

To me, one of the most rewarding aspects about successfully hiring reformed ex-offenders is that you can work with a highly reputable organization that rehabilitates ex-offenders. Usually, the organization has a staff member who is responsible for job placement. This person has a great feel for the clients who are ready to enter the workforce. Again, always make sure you interview potential candidates face to face. And, of course, conduct a thorough background check to ensure you're taking all the necessary steps to protect the new employee and your organization.

Hiring reformed ex-offenders is a great resource for potential great employees and can also be used as a marketing tool for your customers and prospects. It's great PR, because you're giving back to your community. What better way than to give people a second chance at life?

People with special needs

Another great employment resource to tap into is hiring special-needs employees. Depending on their disability, they can excel at a wide variety of jobs. I have had a great deal of luck working with autistic, hearing impaired, and handicapped individuals. I find them highly capable of doing many tasks with a great deal of commitment and pride in their work.

I recommend contacting local, state, and national organizations that support the special-needs community. The National Autism Association is a great resource. Once again, you need to conduct thorough vetting and face-to-face interviews with these folks. Understand their limitations and their requirements. Work with many nonprofit organizations, so you have this resource to tap into when opportunities come along to hire these individuals.

Consider hiring Second Chancers and those who have been left behind

Tapping into these resources gives these folks the opportunity to work, and can help your bottom line. They do not demand high salaries, they are usually very reliable, and they take pride in their jobs. Furthermore, it will give your business a great reputation as a company that gives back to the community and helps people. And most important, you're giving these folks a chance to work and prosper and, at the same time, it gives you another recruitment resource.

Chapter 3

Learning to build a viable business

I went to school for hotel management at Johnson & Wales University in Providence, Rhode Island. I was an okay student. I wasn't the best; I wasn't the worst. I was more interested in the social aspect of college than the curriculum aspect. Hotel management people tend to be pretty social – we aren't the brightest or the most studious. We were the likeable guys; the ones who got invited to all the parties. We learned to lean on our likeability factor and our ability to build relationships with people to get us through school.

During our senior year, hotel and hospitality companies such as Hilton, The Ritz-Carlton, Hyatt, and TGI Fridays came to the school to recruit. I really wanted to work for Hyatt. It's one of the leading hotel companies in the world, plus the organization's philosophy on managing a hotel was unusually entrepreneurial.

Unlike other hotel companies, Hyatt empowered its managers to run their hotels as if they were their own business. There were no standard operating procedures. Managers were given guidelines and pro formas (how they wanted you to perform), but Hyatt corporate headquarters left it up to the hotel's management team to determine how to get there.

Plus, Hyatt's corporate training program was second to none. I really connected to the Hyatt vibe, and I was determined to become a corporate management trainee. However, Hyatt required a minimum 3.0 grade point average for recruits to be accepted in its management program. I only had a 2.8 GPA. When I first tried to get an interview, I got turned down, because I didn't have the grades. Instead of taking no for an answer and moving on, I decided to work around the system.

It turned out I was friends with the career advisor's girlfriend. I went to her and explained the situation, saying that I really wanted an interview with Hyatt but her boyfriend had turned me down because of my GPA.

"Let me see what I can do," she said. It worked. He added my name in an open slot on the interview schedule. The appointment was early, and he said my chances of actually getting the job were slim to none, but at least I was on the schedule.

I'll never forget that interview. I lived about a mile away from campus with several other guys in the hotel management program. I had to walk, first thing in the morning, to meet with Hyatt. I put on my suit and started walking. It was the middle of February, there was nearly two feet of snow on the ground, and it was twenty degrees outside. When I arrived for the interview, my face was red, and the bottom of my pants and my shoes were soaking wet. I didn't look like an A-plus guy! But I nailed the interview anyway. The recruiter asked me questions, and it really seemed like I blew her away with my answers. But Hyatt only had 600 corporate management trainee positions available, and they interviewed thousands and thousands of students across the nation. The only reason I got the interview in the first place was to fill an empty slot on the interview schedule. There was no chance I would get the job. But I left the interview feeling really good.

Meanwhile, I also interviewed with other companies that were recruiting students in the hotel management program. Plus, six of my eight roommates interviewed with Hyatt. Fast forward a couple of weeks, and the offers started coming in. I received offers to work for The Ritz-Carlton, TGI Fridays, and Stouffer's. But I was waiting for that Hyatt offer. Even though they only paid $16,000 a year to be a corporate management trainee, I wanted that job.

One day, my six roommates all got rejection letters from Hyatt, but I didn't. I was the only one who didn't get that letter. I wondered what was going on. After a couple of days, I couldn't wait anymore. I called Hyatt's corporate office and asked to speak to the recruiter who'd interviewed me. It felt like I was on hold for an eternity, but it was probably more like thirty seconds. When she picked up, I explained that I was following up on my interview.

"Steve, congratulations," she said. "We would love to have you as one of our management corporate trainees."

I actually got the job! This was one of the best days of my life. I couldn't believe it. I was one of only four students at my college who received an offer from Hyatt. I was so excited. Up to this point, I had only visualized what I wanted my career to look like; now it was becoming a reality.

I always considered myself to be a hardworking person. My parents paid my tuition and board, but I worked a part-time job as a room service waiter to help offset my college expenses and avoid being a starving student. I worked hard, never knowing whether things would work out the way I wanted. Getting hired at one of the most recognizable hotel companies in the world felt like everything was falling into place. I may not have been the smartest person academically, but I was able to use my life experiences, my tenacity, and my passion to get the *one* job I had set my sights on. At that moment, I realized these traits set me apart from the other students.

Hyatt gave me three choices. I could train in Houston, Miami, or New Orleans. And they needed a decision pretty quickly. I had been to Miami but not Houston or New Orleans. I chose Houston, because this city had four sports teams I'm a huge sports fan. I graduated in May and started August 1 at the Hyatt

Regency Houston, ready to start on my career path to success and the next chapter of my life.

During my early years at Hyatt, I learned what it meant to be a good employee. The training program lasted a year and taught me all the different aspects of a hotel. You spend time working in the food-and-beverage department, the rooms division, sales, accounting, and human resources. After you've experienced all the different departments, you choose one department. I decided to concentrate on the rooms division, which encompasses housekeeping, the front office, guest services, and transportation.

My first position was assistant executive housekeeper. After six or seven months, I was promoted to the front office. My typical hours, unfortunately, were 7:00 p.m. to 7:00 a.m. I was general manager of Hyatt Regency Houston during the graveyard shift! It was really hard, but I was dedicated. I knew if I put in the hard work – the blood, sweat, and tears – I could move up the ladder with this company.

One night, about 1:00 a.m., a hotel guest came to the front desk, frantic, because he'd left his dress shoes at home. He had an important business presentation in the morning, and he only had a pair of sneakers. He was distraught and asked where he could buy a pair of black shoes at that time of night. Nothing in Houston was open, so I gave him the only solution I had.

"You can borrow mine if you want," I said. "I'll be done with work by then anyway."

"What shoe size are you?" he asked.

"I'm a nine."

"That's my size!" The next morning, he came to the front desk, and I gave him my black dress shoes. I didn't mind, because I could walk across the parking lot and drive home in my socks. Having a pair of shoes would make this guy's day. When he returned to the hotel, he left them at the desk for me.

Two weeks later, the general manager called me into his office and said, "I just got a letter about you from Darryl Hartley-Leonard, the CEO of Hyatt."

It turned out my shoes helped this guest secure a $5 million deal. He wrote an amazing letter to the CEO about how Steve Scher was an exemplary employee of Hyatt, and they should be proud to have me on their team. In his letter, he explained how I gave him the shoes off my feet, so he could give his presentation. He said, from now on, he would only stay at Hyatt hotels. The CEO of Hyatt received the guest's letter and wrote to my boss about what an outstanding job I'd done.

This small favor got so much attention. Not long after that, the corporate office called to offer me a position as the opening assistant executive housekeeper for a new Hyatt Regency in Burlingame, California.

I remember saying, "Burlingame? Isn't that in Vermont?" Houston was as far west as I'd ever been.

"No, Burlington is in Vermont. Burlingame is near San Francisco," he said. So why not? I accepted the offer. But this call came on Thursday, and the job started on Monday.

At the time, I was living with my college sweetheart in Houston. Three days later, I left on a plane, and she had to pack up the apartment and drive to San Francisco.

In those days, if you were asked to open a new hotel, it was a big deal. Being part of the opening team was different than transferring to an existing hotel, because you were responsible for creating the culture. You were responsible for setting up all the systems and procedures within your department and hiring all the staff. It was a huge feather in my cap, because opening a hotel is a huge project.

I had no idea what to expect. I showed up for my first day of work in a suit. Everyone else was wearing jeans and sweatshirts, because the hotel was dirty and unfinished. They hadn't even put in credenzas or set up the guest rooms. It really was still under construction. And the place had 791 rooms! This was a much bigger project than I anticipated, but the entire team embraced it.

My team – one executive housekeeper and two assistant executive housekeepers – were literally working behind the construction crew. As soon as the crew finished an area of the hotel, our housekeeping team went in and cleaned it. At this point, the hotel staff consisted solely of managers. There weren't any employees yet. That phase went on for about two months. Once everything was built and cleaned, we started staging the hotel, which meant setting up the guest rooms' furniture and décor. Then we started interviewing and hiring the staff, which took another month.

Next, we trained the new employees and finished the guest rooms. We arranged furniture, made beds, and put in amenities. We were working from 7:00 a.m. to midnight every day. It was so invigorating. There's something to be said about helping to transform the shell of a building into a beautiful, state-of-the-art hotel. It was the first time I experienced company camaraderie, teamwork, and total accomplishment. The managers and employees all came together with the same goal in mind: create a beautiful hotel. Working so hard together created a special bond among us. And from this, we created an unbelievable culture that helped launch the hotel to immediate success.

By the time we opened, we were exhausted. But we were so proud of what we had accomplished. We referred to this as being *Hyattized*. We held a grand opening and got such a positive response from the community and our guests. The hotel was busy, and it stayed busy. I got really tight with the housekeeping team and everyone else who worked in the hotel. We became one big, happy family. After about six months, I was promoted to executive housekeeper.

And then the unthinkable happened. Just six months after we opened, a big earthquake hit San Francisco. I was in my office and had just posted the new work schedule, so I had a line of housekeepers at my door trying to make schedule changes. My parents had been visiting me – I'd put them in our best room, the grand suite, and they'd just left earlier that day. The hotel was fully booked, because the San Francisco Giants and Oakland A's were playing a World Series game. When the earthquake happened, most of the guests were on their way to the baseball game.

Everything started shaking. I had no idea what was happening. I was from New Jersey – what did I know about earthquakes? But my employees were looking at me, wondering what to do. I knew we had to get everyone out of the building as fast as possible, so we all started moving toward the front door. I remember it took a while, because several doors were jammed shut. Finally, we got everyone outside – guests and employees. I looked up at the building and saw that the grand suite, where my parents had been just hours before, was destroyed.

Soon after, the general manager and I went to every room to check for people who might still be inside. On the seventh floor, I opened a room with my master key and found a woman, in shock, sitting on the bed. She was a flight attendant – our hotel was right next to the airport. She couldn't move. I had to help her stand up, walk down seven flights of stairs, and escort her through the lobby and out the front door.

At this point, everyone was still so scared and in the dark about the severity of the earthquake. It was chaos. At one point, one of the hotel telephone operators asked if I could take a call from Darryl Hartley-Leonard, because the general manager was busy. I grabbed the phone and was on the line with the CEO of Hyatt. He had all the top executives in his office in Chicago, wanting to know what was going on.

"What's your name?" he asked.

"Steve Scher."

"Steve Scher? Aren't you the guy who gave the guest the shoes off your feet a couple of years ago?"

"Yeah, that's me." I told him we'd gotten everyone out of the rooms, and the building had sustained a lot of structural damage. I didn't know the extent, but I knew it wasn't good. In fact, I could walk down one of the corridors upstairs and see the water features in the lobby through the crack in the floor. The hotel had been built on a landfill, and it moved sixteen inches during the quake.

In those days, no one had cell phones. But one person had a car phone. He and his wife took names of everyone who wanted to reach out to their families to let them know they were safe, including me. My mom and stepdad were on an airplane flying back to New Jersey when the earthquake hit. During the flight, the pilot announced that there had just been a devastating earthquake in San Francisco. I found out that my mom read the same page in her book for two hours, because she was so worried.

At the hotel, everything was a mess. Guests began returning, and we had about 2,000 people milling around the lobby and ballroom, because the fire chief wouldn't let anyone go upstairs. We took all the food from the walk-in refrigerators, grabbed all the alcohol from the bar, and threw a party for our guests and employees. Our tight-knit Hyatt family grew even tighter that day.

The hotel sustained over $24 million in damage and closed down for two years, so it could be rebuilt. Hyatt assigned me to several other projects during those two years. My general manager in Burlingame was promoted to general manager of Hyatt's flagship property, Hyatt Regency Chicago, and he took me with him for about four months to improve their housekeeping department.

When that project was done, they sent me to Park Hyatt Beaver Creek Resort & Spa to open that Colorado hotel. Next, they transferred me to Hyatt Palm Springs in California (a hotel Hyatt had purchased and was preparing to reopen). I got a lot of experience during those two years. When "my" building was ready, I went back to Burlingame and back to my duties as executive housekeeper.

Those years were pivotal, because I learned so much about building a business. I learned how to manage people, about creating a great culture, and about the politics of working with different departments. At many hotel companies, everything was done according to huge manuals of standard operating procedures. Corporate headquarters told you exactly how to do everything, step by step. Hyatt gave us the tools, but we had to figure out how to build and manage the hotel. We got to make decisions, build vendor relationships, and figure out everything from staff security to linens and soap. I got to practice entrepreneurship over and over again on Hyatt's dime.

Not every lesson was easy to learn, though. I was named Manager of the Quarter, and I got accolades and recognition from many top executives. But I let that go to my head, and I learned an important lesson because of it. As far as my superiors were concerned, I could do no wrong. The general manager was taking me to baseball games and giving me preferential treatment. But other managers – my peers – resented me. They thought I was arrogant and cocky and unapproachable. I didn't know this until my general manager brought me into his office one day.

"Steve," he said, "I want to give you the Manager of the Year Award. You deserve it. You've done a great job helping to reopen this hotel. But I can't give the award to you, because your line-level managers hate you."

This devastated me. I had no idea; I thought I was the guy everyone liked. That day, I realized the importance of making every experience you have with everyone a great experience. You have to treat everyone with respect. That was a real kick in the butt for me, but I learned a critical lesson that would serve me throughout my career.

I was with Hyatt for eight years. Even though I was an employee, I really learned to think like an entrepreneur. I believe that as entrepreneurs we are really "Architects." We have the vision, and we have to surround ourselves with "Builders" who can see our vision and help make that vision a reality.

I learned from this experience that if you can get people to trust you, believe in you, and believe in your vision, you'll be successful. I learned that creating a positive culture is the foundation to a successful business. I learned that when you build a strong team based on trust and mutual respect, you can do almost anything. Although I didn't know it at the time, I was able to catapult that experience into my own business efforts. It was great training to learn how to do my own thing. And when it was time to build my own business, this experience inspired me to think big.

Chapter 4

Reinvesting, thinking bigger, and creating culture

Early in my career at Hyatt, I learned to think like an entrepreneur, and I learned to think big. Not long after purchasing Acrobat Outsourcing – and after the hospital strike ended – I had what many business owners can only dream of having: $1 million to reinvest into the business. I had big plans and dreams of growing this small temporary staffing agency into a national player. And I had the capital to do it.

Plus, the work felt really good. I liked helping people find jobs, especially the temporary employees we recruited who were formally incarcerated, were recovering addicts, or had special needs. All their lives, these men and women had been told they were no good. The only way they had earned a living was by hustling it on the streets. This time they did it the right way. You could see it in their eyes – the confidence they had as they were telling me how they felt and what they planned to do with the money they earned. I can't begin to tell you how many of these employees thanked me for getting them a job. They were able to buy Christmas gifts for their kids. They felt proud. I loved being a part of that transformation in their lives. I couldn't have been happier for them.

And I was thrilled that the hospital strike was finally over. I had worked twenty hours a day for nine weeks straight. I had been putting out fires left and right, constantly recruiting and replacing temp workers due to attrition. I was exhausted. I even lost twenty pounds, because there was no time to eat. It was the hardest nine weeks of my life.

I was sitting on a million dollars in cash. Most entrepreneurs would never be in this situation. It was epic. I felt like the luckiest guy in the world. But there was a downside. As soon as I stopped staffing the hospital strike, I realized my other business was minimal. My annual revenue fell to $200,000 – a drop in the bucket compared to what we had just accomplished.

Cashing out never crossed my mind, but if I wanted to grow the business, I needed a plan. Luckily, I now had a pot of gold to work with to grow and reinvent my business.

My first decision was to get out of the Tenderloin. Every time I parked and got out of my car, I'd be panhandled or someone would try to sell me drugs. I often had to kick people out of my doorway, because they'd slept there overnight. I needed a more convenient location for employees to come for interviews in a safe location that didn't embarrass me or scare anyone away. I needed an office I could be proud to call Acrobat Outsourcing headquarters.

I spent two weeks on my feet, going to every neighborhood in San Francisco looking for the right place. I liked the Mission Bay/South Park area, which was up-and-coming at the time. The San Francisco Giants played about a block away, so the area was transitioning into a hot spot. I found an office that was located near a bus stop and train station. In fact, every method of public transportation in San Francisco stopped near or right in front of this office building. When I saw this office, I knew it would be the new home of Acrobat Outsourcing.

However, moving to a nicer and more convenient neighborhood came with a considerable rent increase. I went from paying $800 a month in the Tenderloin to $2,500 a month in the new location. But this new location helped our recruiting tremendously. It was convenient for temporary staff people to get there, and it attracted better internal employees, because people wanted to work in this area. When customers came to my office, the place represented my vision of what Acrobat could be and eventually would be.

Now, with a new location, I started investing the profits from the strike back into the company. Most temporary foodservice staffing companies are mom-and-pop shops working out of their homes, providing jobs for friends and family. Even Acrobat, when I bought it, was a small operation that just provided extra wait staff for hotels or a replacement cook to cover a breakfast shift. I was thinking on a much, much bigger scale. I wanted to take this business mainstream. I wanted to create a company that would have a national presence. I wanted to go big.

That means I needed to be in markets that would sustain Monday through Friday business. This was important for keeping temporary employees working and building up our roster of temp employees. In this business, Monday through Friday work is your bread and butter. I started executing my vision by looking at all our potential markets – any venue that provided foodservice. I broke these venues into different types of verticals:

1. Corporate cafeterias – I wanted to provide all types of staffing inside a corporate cafeteria: cooks, dishwashers, servers, cashiers, and baristas.

2. Colleges and universities – I wanted to staff college cafeterias, college event centers, college stadiums, and fraternity and sorority houses.

3. Sports and entertainment venues – Being a huge sports and concert fan, I wanted to provide concessionaires, cashiers, cooks, and prep cooks to all the stadiums and venues in our area.

4. Hospitals and rehabilitation centers – I wanted to provide cooks, dishwashers, and tray line servers to hospital and rehab cafeterias.

5. Caterers and country clubs – I wanted to provide cooks, servers, and bartenders. I wanted to be involved in every catered party in San Francisco.

6. Private parties – I saw opportunities to staff all types of catered private parties relating to charitable fundraisers, holiday events, political fundraisers, and more.

San Francisco offered numerous potential customers in all these verticals, and I wanted to start building relationships with as many of them as I could.

I needed people to help me get my ideas off the ground and make my vision a reality. During the hospital strike, my internal staff consisted of just Rhonda and Johnny Diego. Rhonda moved to Chicago and, after the strike, I kept Johnny as an internal staff member, because he was so dedicated and so good at his job. I promoted him to full-time staffing manager. He received custody of his baby, and was being recognized by the prison system as the "poster child" for reformed ex-offenders who are creating success in their lives. To help Johnny and me, I hired six more people.

From my years at Hyatt, I learned about building a great culture. When it was time to build Acrobat, I knew culture was essential. A huge part of this is finding the right people. When hiring someone, I rely heavily on my gut instinct. I have to like them enough to be able to sit down and have a beer together. They might not have all the experience in the world, but if they have the intangibles – the likeability factor and I can see that they're a good person – then I'll want to hire them. I'll want to mentor them, and spend time with them, so they'll continue to grow.

One of the people I hired was actually a supervisor at the hospital during the strike. Shasta was responsible for managing a lot of the Acrobat temp employees at the hospital, and I was impressed with her. She was charismatic, gregarious, smart, sweet, and kind. She had no experience in staffing, but she had the intangibles of being a good person and good employee: hardworking, loyal to the core, thinks outside the box, entrepreneurial spirit, wants to do great things, and totally likable. I am about treating people with respect and earning respect, and that's an important part of what I look for.

Then I hired a sales manager. Caterina was a go-getter salesperson who was great at her job. She knew the fine line between being aggressive and getting the deal done. (If you're too aggressive, customers will think you're a pain in the neck.)

My top recruiter was a very likable young man. He believed in my vision and was a great soul. And I hired a woman who was fresh out of college, looking to start her career. We had an eclectic group of people, but the energy worked. We were all excited about building a great company. The culture I envisioned was starting to take shape.

I sat down with the sales team and said, "All right, guys. This year is about building the company. Here's our plan." We had to see Acrobat as a sales company that happened to provide temporary staffing services. No matter what service we provide, the lights don't come on and nobody gets paid if we don't have sales. Each sales employee was assigned to a vertical. I spent $50,000 on marketing. We targeted accounts, started building relationships with customers, and started penetrating the different verticals.

The rest of my team (including myself) focused on recruiting temp employees and building a roster of qualified temps to send on work assignments. We cultivated relationships with every culinary school, career center, halfway house, and vocational school in the area. I realized that we needed to recruit and sell at the same time. If you have temp jobs you can't staff because you don't have employees, you'll lose the customer. If you have temp employees ready to work, but no job assignments for them, then you'll lose qualified temp employees. It was critical to have both engines running at the same time.

During that year, we revamped our recruiting, hiring, and temporary employee development. As we picked up more accounts, we needed a roster of really good people to fill the jobs. We had been relying on online classified ads such as Craigslist to attract workers, but that would never bring enough people through the door. I put one of my employees in charge of recruiting and tasked him with cultivating relationships with potential hires throughout San Francisco, San Jose, and Sacramento.

When I took an objective look at my business, Acrobat Outsourcing had two different customers: The companies buying our services and the temp workers filling the jobs. We were working hard to get customers to use our services, so I put the same effort into our recruiting strategies to find great temp employees.

The best temp employees we found were people who had full-time jobs in foodservice and were interested in picking up extra shifts. They're great employees, because they're reliable, hardworking, and experienced. However, they have a full-time job. That's their priority; temp jobs aren't their priority.

The second-best type was college students. A lot of students look for ways to make money, and temporary staffing is often ideal for them, because it's flexible. When they're on break or they have a day off, they can work temp jobs. The problem with hiring students is, once again, working a temp job is not their top priority. If they have a test or a party they want to go to, they call out, leaving us in a scramble to find a replacement.

The third-best type was stay-at-home moms looking for extra work. These women are reliable, great employees, and often have relevant work experience. Again, there is a downside: If their child is sick, they call out. Often, they had to be off work by 3:00 p.m., so they could pick up their kids from school.

All three types of temp employees tend to have tight availability, and working for my company was not their main priority. To serve our customers, I needed to build a large roster of good, reliable employees who could work at all hours, day or night. We soon realized that some of the most reliable people came from halfway houses, transitional housing, and clean-and-sober living facilities. These people have to sign in, sign out, and state exactly where they're going. They're always looking to get out of the house for the day, gain experience, and earn money.

We started building relationships with different types of clean-and-sober living facilities, rehab facilities, halfway houses, nonprofits, and other organizations focused on getting people back on their feet and back into society. We spent a great deal of effort cultivating relationships with these different organizations. That's when our recruiting efforts really started gaining momentum.

I also knew I wanted to expand Acrobat into new locations. Based on what I learned about doing business in San Francisco, I knew there were certain metrics that a location had to meet to make it a viable market. First, I needed cities with an abundance of opportunities that can keep my employees working Monday through Friday. Cities with a large number of corporate cafeterias meet that criterion. Second, I looked for cities that had lots of colleges and hospitals in the area, since these have cafeterias as well. Third, I looked at the social aspect of the city. Are there many caterers, country clubs, entertainment venues, and stadiums?

The first expansion city I chose was San Jose. It met the metrics. In particular, there was a huge presence of corporate cafeterias. Companies such as Apple, Cisco, and Google had headquarters in or near San Jose. Also, the city was home to many colleges and universities including Santa Clara University, San Jose State University, and Stanford University. This area is also home of the San Francisco 49ers and San Jose Sharks. So this choice made perfect sense.

What Silicon Valley is to San Jose, government business is to Sacramento. I chose Sacramento as a second expansion city, because it offered a lot of government-related business we could staff through the five-day work week. And there are sports teams, colleges, and hospitals in the surrounding area. Plus, there are plenty of country clubs, caterers, private parties, and other social-event business. I rented two offices in shared workspaces to have a physical presence in both areas. Now Acrobat Outsourcing was operating in San Francisco, San Jose, and Sacramento.

The other big investment I wanted to make was implementing a software system that would track every aspect of my business. We had been doing everything manually with Excel spreadsheets. I wanted to buy a state-of-the-art software system that would keep track of my recruiting efforts, temp employees, customers, payroll, billing, and accounts receivables. I spent weeks looking for an off-the-shelf product that would fit our needs.

I bought a software program for about $100,000. But it was not a good solution for Acrobat. After three months of working on this system, trying to make it fit our business processes and business flow, I realized it just wouldn't work. Acrobat is a niche business, and no off-the-shelf product could ever do what we needed it to do. We needed something custom built.

It turned out that Shasta's dad helped to build the software program for AT&T's online phone billing system. He was close to retirement and agreed to build a customized office system for us. Scrapping the software I'd spent so much money on was a tough decision, but the custom system we built was a perfect, easy-to-use, web-based solution with all the features I wanted. I could be sitting on the beach in Tahiti, pull up the system, and look at my numbers for the week. I could see if I was profitable or not. A calendar showed who was on a job, who wasn't on a job, what jobs needed to be filled, and what jobs were already filled. All the temp employees had a timesheet in the system, so they could sign in and out. We also included an evaluation form, so customers could rate the quality of the temp employee on a scale of one to five.

We spent about six months building this system, and it cost me about $75,000. But it was customized, robust, and easy to use. And it differentiated us from our competitors. As the owner, I had the power of information. When you have information about every aspect of your company, it allows you to make sound business decisions.

While we were working on this system, we had a hard time coming up with a name for it. We sat there, my entire team, and brainstormed what to call it. We came up with a lot of different names. Finally, the name *Taborca* popped into my head, because it's *Acrobat* spelled backward. Everyone loved it. So that was the birth of Taborca – my custom-built, enterprise software system that improved productivity, gave me a snapshot of my business anytime I needed it, and kept track of everything.

That year, we implemented Taborca, we built the website, we had the marketing going, and Acrobat Outsourcing started growing. Unfortunately, during the strike, we had developed a reputation for supplying nothing more than a warm body to the companies who used our services. After all, I did have Larry (the guy I fired) badmouthing me, so he could get my business. Although I had few complaints from my customers, my competitors said terrible things about the employees we sent to fill jobs. I knew this smear campaign about my temp employees wasn't true, but I needed to prove it.

I wanted to grow these employees and really let them differentiate Acrobat from our competitors. I came up with a strategy. First, I gave everyone who applied for a temp job a skills test with fifteen multiple-choice questions about their experience. Servers took a serving test, bartenders took a bartending test, and so forth. We needed to clearly understand their skillset. Those with a lot of experience aced the test. A lot of temp employees failed the test miserably, because they were really just looking for a job – any job. They'd sign up for anything, whether they knew what they were doing or not.

That's when I decided to start Acrobat Academy– a hands-on training program for new and existing temp employees who wanted to hone their skills or learn new skills. This helped our people grow. And it became a value proposition for potential temp employees to choose Acrobat over our competitors. This gave them experience and training, and they could leverage these skills into more money and better positions. Plus, it also made them more valuable to Acrobat and, subsequently, to our customers. This improved our reputation and differentiated us from our competitors.

Once a week, Acrobat Academy held classes on different topics. We had server training classes for employees who applied for serving positions. Many didn't even know the correct way to set a table. We put tables in the conference room and practiced serving from the right, clearing from the left, carrying trays, and other skills they would need in serving positions. We did hands-on cook training to work on knife skills and food handling.

The greatest aspect of these training programs was helping employees who started in low-level roles such as a dishwasher move up, through the kitchen ranks, into positions such as prep cook and grill cook. They could make more money, and this gave them an opportunity to make themselves more marketable for other temporary and full-time positions that came available through Acrobat Outsourcing.

That year, our biggest break came when one of our customers, the Academy of Art University in San Francisco, started using our temporary staffing services for their cafeteria. Then another account, the San Ramon Valley Conference Center, started using a lot of our people for their cafeteria. A large company called Sodexo USA managed both cafeterias. Sodexo is a foodservice company that manages cafeterias in colleges, corporations, and hospitals around the nation. When Sodexo noticed it was sending Acrobat a lot of checks, the company approached us about being a preferred vendor.

Becoming a preferred vendor meant we were given a "hunting license" to go after any Sodexo account in San Francisco, San Jose, and Sacramento. The company gave us a list of its cafeterias in those three cities. Every Acrobat salesperson got that list, and we went after every one of those locations, really working hard to get our name into these Sodexo accounts. And it started working. We went from $5,000 a week of Sodexo business to about $15,000 a week.

The second break we got that year was with The Gap. The corporate headquarters is located in San Francisco, and the company has different locations for teams that manage The Gap, Old Navy, and Banana Republic. The three cafeterias were self-run, meaning they weren't using a company like Sodexo to manage their foodservice operations. When The Gap decided it only wanted to manage – and not staff – the cafeterias, it looked for an outside company to provide all the foodservice staff. We went through a request for proposal and negotiation process, and we won the account.

The work we were doing started snowballing. Now we had some momentum in San Francisco, but I still needed to get the San Jose and Sacramento offices off the ground.

Our first break in San Jose was Google. I owe this one to my salesperson in San Jose. One of my favorite sayings is "Persistence overcomes resistance," and this woman was practically sleeping on Google's doorstep. She was determined to work with Google. This went on for weeks. Then one day, we got a call from Google.

"All right," they said. "Caterina has been here every day, and we're going to give you guys a shot."

We started by staffing one or two employees at Google. That quickly became five to ten employees a day. Then we got the Google summer picnic, an annual employee event where they turn the campus into an amusement park. They wanted us to provide all the staff for the event – about 200 temp employees. That was our largest single-day event to date. We recruited the staff, staffed the event, and it was great. We became Google's preferred vendor, and the company used us all the time after that.

Then we landed the San Francisco Giants account. We started providing concessionaires and cashiers for their home games. It started out small. We had to prove ourselves. We started by bringing in ten to twenty-five temp employees per home game, and that grew to fifty to seventy-five temp employees per game. Now, our San Francisco office was on a roll, and San Jose was strong with Google.

We established ourselves in Sacramento when we got a large country club called Haggin Oaks Golf Complex that needed staff for social events, weddings, golf parties, and reunions. As soon as word got out that there was a new staffing company in Sacramento, I got a call from a guy who said he had an agreement with the former Acrobat owner. He claimed they had agreed Acrobat would never come to Sacramento and his company would never go to San Francisco. He said I was breaking a long-standing agreement between the two companies to stay off each other's turf.

If such an agreement existed, it had nothing to do with me. And I explained this to him. He said, "Well, then, I'm coming to San Francisco to compete against you."

"John," I said, "There's enough business for both of us. Come to San Francisco." I truly believe that competition is good for a business. And that's what he did, and my business didn't suffer. Despite the fact that his company was the "800-pound gorilla" in Sacramento, we landed a few accounts and started gaining momentum there. By the end of the year, we had three well-established offices and $2 million in sales.

The funniest call I got that year was from Larry, my former employee who started taking accounts when he left. He said, "I underestimated you, Steve. I think if I were to come back to Acrobat, I would close my company, and you and I could conquer the entire country together. I'll be your right-hand man. Make me a partner, and we'll be extremely successful."

I can't repeat the first words that came out of my mouth! But this was my first chance to unload on this guy, who I'd considered public enemy number one for months. He took Acrobat accounts and bad-mouthed me all over town. Six months after that call, he was out of business. I'm a firm believer in karma, so I didn't feel bad that he went out of business. Furthermore, that was one competitor I didn't need to worry about anymore.

The money I made from the hospital strike redefined Acrobat. Reinvesting the profits allowed me to grow Acrobat from a small mom-and-pop staffing operation to an established business with three locations and a roster of high-profile customers. The investments and strategic growth redefined us and helped to lay the foundation for what Acrobat was to become.

On-target business advice

How to make technology work for you and your bottom line

In this day and age, it's imperative that entrepreneurs take advantage of available technology. Having the power of information at your fingertips can give you an advantage over your competitors and, by the same token, can help save money for your bottom line.

However, there's a fine line between implementing too much technology or not enough. I believe that in order to have a successful business there needs to be a level of customer and employee contact, so you're able to manage your business and continue to cultivate relationships. When consulting, I tell my clients to stay updated on all technology that's available to streamline your business and save you money.

Customer relationship management (CRM) system

Back in the day, companies relied on keeping track of their business by hand. It was extremely time consuming and hard to stay on top of all the details. As years went by and technology started to emerge, we were introduced to Microsoft Office. Businesses and entrepreneurs started using Excel spreadsheets and Word docs to keep track of their business. But as technology continued to evolve, many off-the-shelf CRM systems became available. These systems specialized in many different industries and tried to become a one-size-fits-all solution. Problem is, no two companies are exactly alike. I urge my clients to evaluate as many systems as they can (and have time for) in order to find the right system for their company.

I can't stress enough how important it is to have a CRM system that works in synch with your business flow. This decision will be one of the most critical decisions you make as an entrepreneur. It must be user-friendly and capture as much data as you need in order to make sound business decisions. And you'll need to get buy-in from your employees. In addition, I recommend you find a web-based system. This means you can access it anywhere in the world, so you can always get a snapshot of your business no matter where you are. I also recommend you are absolutely certain about the system you choose. It can be detrimental if you choose the wrong system, because it can ultimately have a negative effect on your company's productivity.

If you can't find the right system, I would explore investing in a customized CRM system. Today, it's not hard to find developers at a reasonable rate to help you build one that meets all of your business criteria. I learned the hard way. When I first started my company, I feverishly looked for a system that would meet my business needs. After much research, I settled for an off-the-shelf product that only met about seventy-five percent of my business needs. After a while it became apparent that the system I chose was flawed, because it only gave me about seventy-five percent of the data and insight I needed.

I scrapped that software, and I decided to invest in a customized solution. It was one of the best decisions I made, because it captured everything I was looking for: complete business data and resulting insights.

Telephone: VoIP versus traditional landlines

When you're looking for phone systems for your business, you have two choices: VoIP (voice over Internet protocol) or a traditional landline. VoIP is known as Internet calling. You use your Internet connection to make calls, and your voice is transmitted as data over the Internet. A landline telephone is connected to the phone network via copper wires or fiber optic. Although landlines are reliable, this tends to be expensive and not very feature rich. With VoIP, you can use your mobile phone, computer, or desk phone to make calls. In addition, this option gives you more control of the phone experience. There are many reasons why VoIP is the choice I recommend to my clients. Here are some of the features and benefits:

- You don't have to be in your office to make or receive phone calls.

- Key features include auto-attendants, call forwarding, call recording, call analytics, voicemail-to-email messaging, voicemail-to-text, and anonymous call rejection.

- Softphone capability means that, essentially, you can turn any device into a phone including your mobile device, tablet, and laptop.

- VoIP phone systems can be integrated with several third-party tools and software such as your CRM tool, sales software, or email marketing software.

- VoIP allows for scalability, since adding lines doesn't require on-premise changes. The best thing about switching to VoIP is that you'll see a significant savings on your phone bill, which will have a direct impact on your bottom line.

Productivity

One of the most expensive costs you will endure as an entre-preneur is lack of productivity from your employees. There's no way to actually measure how much money you're los-ing based on lack of productivity, but I guarantee that if you don't provide employees with the correct tools they need to do their job, you're losing a substantial amount of revenue. As an example, I always provided my employees with a lap-top computer, an extra monitor, cellphone, and a comfortable work area. It was my goal as their leader to ensure they had everything they needed to be productive and comfortable in their work environment.

Be in the know

Be relentless in your pursuit to educate yourself on emerg-ing technologies and how they relate to your business. New products are launched throughout the year, and you owe it to yourself to keep up with these technologies to learn how they could improve your business. Subscribe to your trade associa-tions' publications and trade magazines – use these vehicles to keep up with industry trends and innovations. You owe it to yourself.

Chapter 5

The business of people

Fear motivates me, and I think this is true for many entrepreneurs. I always feared that if I wasn't working continuously every day to build my business, it would all go away. That's the way my mind worked. Even though I was doing $1 million or $2 million in sales – and we were making a name for ourselves – I always feared that if I don't staff this next job, my business will go away. However, I could never do all the work myself. I needed a team, and I wanted to lead by example.

Culture allows you to get people to buy into your business philosophy, buy into your vision, and buy into your growth. My success at Acrobat Outsourcing comes down to my team and the fact that I built a culture that got the most out of my employees. Make them part of the process, part of the team, so they feel like they're a huge contributor and not just an hourly or salaried employee.

I also wanted my employees to have some skin in the game. I gave my internal employees a base salary, plus a commission on everything they sold and quarterly bonus opportunities that were a stretch but were achievable. That way, you get them to buy into your vision, buy into your business, and continue to grow the business because they feel a part of it. And if they feel a part of it, they'll work harder. In my business, the phone could ring at all hours of the day or night. It was imperative that an employee was on call to answer those phone calls.

Usually, the calls were from temporary employees calling in sick and needing to be replaced, or the calls were from customers looking for a temporary employee to work that day. If I wanted my employees to fill these last-minute orders – and I did because it was additional revenue into my company and it helped to build trust with my customers – then I had to give them an incentive to do that extra work. We wanted a reputation for reacting fast and filling our customers' needs. If I have to pay an employee a minimal commission to staff that job, it's worth it, because it's either lost revenue that has been recovered or it's new revenue that we didn't expect.

As the business owner, you never want to tell someone to do something you wouldn't normally do. You don't want your employees to think you're taking a free ride on their hard work. Show up and work hard too. Know the answers before anyone else. When I would ask one of my employees a question, I already knew the answer nine out of ten times. I asked the question to find out if they knew the answer. That's not only being an entrepreneur, that's being a leader.

I wanted to know what motivates my employees. I never wanted to get too personal with employees, but I did try to get to know them – whether or not they have a family, what they like to do outside of work, and why they come to work every day. Because when we come to work, we're all in it together. My job as the owner and their boss was to keep them inspired and excited about the work we were doing. I had to continually inspire them, empower them, and help them grow.

One thing I would say to prospective employees when I interviewed them is that it's my responsibility as the leader of the company to make sure the people I hire are better off professionally, financially, and personally a year from when they are hired. If I can't do that, then I have failed, because it's my responsibility to make sure my people grow with the company. At the same time, I have to make sure they are capable of growing with the company. Acrobat grew and evolved quickly, and unfortunately not everyone on that original team was ready for it.

Throughout my career I had employees who were all about creating a buzz and getting business in the door. However, they started having trouble keeping up as we got busier. They refused to work beyond nine-to-five, but in the staffing business, more jobs to staff meant more work. As we got busier, you couldn't work nine-to-five anymore. You had to come in on

Saturdays, and you had to work past 5:00 in the evening, because you had to get jobs staffed. Some people can only go to a certain level. It's as if they hit a ceiling. That means it's time for them to move on, because you need people who can take you to the next level.

I had an employee who got overwhelmed with all the job requests that started coming into our office. When you're hiring temporary staff from all different walks of life, it requires a lot of paperwork. It seemed like everyone we hired had wage garnishments. We needed to fill out all the forms, send them to the city, and orient these new temp employees. There are so many moving parts to this business that it's hard to keep up. She couldn't keep up, so she didn't last very long.

I had another employee who, unbeknownst to me, was turning down business. She was telling customers we couldn't fill temp jobs, because she was so overwhelmed that she didn't want to take on any more job assignments. We had the temporary staff in place. But she hit her ceiling, and I wanted to keep growing.

Letting people go is never easy. But you have to keep your eye on the long game, and keep in mind that every employee makes a contribution to the culture of the business. Some employees might be good for a $1 million company, but can they keep up with a $5 million company, or a $10 million company, or even a $50 million company?

If you want to be successful as an entrepreneur, make sure you have a strong stomach, because you're dealing with something all the time, twenty-four hours a day. People have their drama. And as you get bigger, some people will try to have their hands in your pockets. They think you're a multimillionaire even though you're putting everything into the company. I always had to maintain a high level of vigilance.

But at the same time, I loved the people and the stories I have from my days at Acrobat. By building a good company with a positive culture and strong reputation, we helped people change their lives, because we got them jobs.

As Acrobat's relationship with Google evolved, I started building a great rapport with their foodservice manager. We really trusted each other. One day a young man named Adam came into my office looking for a job. He had received a degree from a culinary academy and wanted to work as a cook or prep cook. But Adam had a handicap. He only had one ear, and he hadn't been able to get a job anywhere. He said, "No one will hire me, because of the way I look."

That broke my heart, and I promised to see what I could do. Later that day I called my contact at Google, Chad, and explained the situation. I said, "I know you guys are looking for prep cooks and cooks, and I have someone for you. He's just looking for a break. Will you take a flyer on this guy and have him be a prep cook at Google?"

Chad hesitated, but I convinced him to find a spot for Adam. He said he could make sandwiches and salads and stock the refrigerators. It paid $12 an hour, and the hours were from 5:00 a.m. to 1:00 p.m. That was the best he could do. But when I told Adam about it, you would've thought he had won the lottery.

"Oh, my god, Steve, I can't believe it," he said. "I'm not going to let you down. I'll do the best job possible."

Adam lived in San Francisco and had to go to Mountain View (Silicon Valley) to work at Google. This is a pretty serious commute for a $12 an hour job, especially one that started at 5:00 in the morning. But on his first day, Adam woke up at 3:00 in the morning, took three buses to get to Mountain View, and made it to work by 5:00 a.m.

I called Chad to check in on Adam that first day. He didn't pick up, so I left a voicemail. But I didn't get a response. Later that week, I called Chad again and left another message.

"Hey," I said. "I understand Adam has been at Google every day this week, but I haven't gotten any feedback. Do you want him to come back next week?" Still no word.

Finally, at 5:00 p.m. on Friday, Chad called and said, "You know, I haven't heard any positive news or negative news. I know he's doing his job, so let's just keep him going for the next week and let me see if I can get some feedback."

Adam worked the next week, once again, getting up at 3:00 in the morning and getting to work by 5:00 a.m. And he kept going in the following week. When I called Chad to see how it was going, he finally had some feedback for me.

"Adam is doing great," he said. "The employees love

him. The managers love him. As a matter of fact, some of the senior executives at Google love him."

Adam worked at Google for another three or four weeks. Then Chad called to tell me again how much they loved working with Adam.

"We want to hire him full time," Chad said. "What is the buyout?"

I said, "Chad, you know what, there is no buyout for Adam. I'm just so happy this kid has a full-time job."

Not only did he have a job, but he had a job at Google, one of the best companies in America. Adam went to work full-time for Google. When I told Adam that Google wanted to offer him a full-time job, he was so emotional. He couldn't have been more appreciative.

I remember another compelling story, which happened during the strike. I was sitting in my office one Saturday morning when one of our temp employees came in for his paycheck. I could tell he was upset. His eyes were like glass. I said, "Ken, what's up? What's going on?"

"My son was just murdered," he said, "and I know who did it. Now I'm going to go take care of it myself."

When he told me that, I was scared out of my mind, because this guy had been to prison, and I had no reason to doubt he would actually go through with it. Not knowing what else to do, I started talking to him about how he didn't really want to do that, because he'd get caught and end up back in prison. I talked to him about letting justice take care of it, which was so difficult since his son had just been murdered that day. We sat there for about two hours, just talking as if we were old friends. Ken and I didn't know each other very well, but I have often wondered what would've happened if I hadn't bothered to ask what was wrong. If he didn't have anyone to talk to who knows what could've happened. But I knew that, as a manager and business owner, I needed to be there for my people. In fact, he was such a good employee that the hospital kept him on after the strike, and he stayed with Acrobat for another two years.

After the strike was over, another man who worked for me named Michael said to me, "Steve, I'm forty years old, and this is the first time I've made an honest living."

Michael was so appreciative that he invited me to his house for dinner. I insisted that he didn't have to do that, but he wouldn't take no for an answer. So one night, around Christmas and just after the hospital strike ended, he instructed me to park near the Candlestick Park stadium. He told me I couldn't park in his neighborhood, because he was afraid my car might get stolen. He picked me up and took me to his apartment.

His apartment was in the government housing projects, where many of my other employees also lived. I ate dinner with his wife and five kids, and the whole time they left their front door ajar. Throughout the meal, neighbors kept stopping by, thanking me for giving their mom, dad, sister, brother, or friend their job opportunity and helping to make Christmas great for them. I felt so happy, but I kept insisting I had nothing to do with their success. I might have given them the opportunity, but they had made the best of it.

During times like these – and I have so many stories – I really understood Acrobat's role in changing people's lives. I remember when I first was contemplating buying the company, I thought it would be a good opportunity to make a decent living. I never realized how powerful putting people to work could be. Giving people jobs affects their livelihood, but it also changes them into more confident people. They earn money doing honest work, they provide for their families, and they feel good about it.

Giving job opportunities to people who made the most of those opportunities is what fueled me. I was proud to place a young man with special needs in one of the top companies in America. And I was proud to place a reformed ex-offender in a hospital where he could start a career and earn a decent living.

Creating a great culture is important to me, because that's what made me successful. That's why people wanted to work for Acrobat. That's why we were able to grow the business. It doesn't matter whether I owned a staffing company or sold widgets. As entrepreneurs, when you build that great culture – whether it's made up of ex-offenders, ex-drug addicts, and people with special needs or it's made up of professionals – you create something that changes people's lives for the better.

On-target business advice

Real-world tips to create a culture of agility and loyalty

If there's one thing entrepreneurs need to focus on during the life cycle of their business it's creating, developing, and maintaining a strong culture. I can't begin to tell you how important company culture is to a business. It's the "vibe" of your business, and it starts with you. You need to be vigilant about maintaining the integrity of the culture. Surround yourself with people who believe in your vision and have the proper toolset to help live your dream.

However, it's not easy to build a strong culture. You need to first take a step back and figure out what you want your company to look like and how you want it to be perceived to your customers and to the public. Remember, perception is reality – and that starts with culture.

I find it remarkable that when I speak to my consulting clients about their business, they want to focus on revenue and profit. Rarely do they inquire about having me help them with their company culture. But I can tell you from first-hand experience that setting the right culture and tone is the most important thing you can do when starting and growing your business.

Whether you're starting your own business or buying an existing business, you have the opportunity to create your own team. When buying an existing business, you have the opportunity of cherry picking current employees on the roster, people who will move forward with you and your business.

When starting anew, you have the ability to build your team from scratch. Here are some tips I learned along the way.

Building your team

Hopefully, you'll come to a point early in your business cycle where you'll need to build out your team. I recommend you start prospecting, interviewing, and hiring your team as soon as you realize you can't manage the business by yourself. Many of my clients wait too long, and they end up quickly hiring someone just to fill a position. Entrepreneurs need to have the foresight to start interviewing candidates before the need arises. Here's the process I recommend:

1. Start getting your feelers out there. Talk to friends, family, and business associates, asking them for recommendations. Place ads on local job boards with your requirements

2. Be specific as to what you are looking for in an employee.

3. Personally interview prospective employees. Take your time during the interview process. Try to get a feel for their skillset, along with their personal interactions. To me, having the right experience is important, but sometimes the intangibles are more important. I look for honesty, loyalty, and commitment. I want someone who has good personal and family values. I try to look inside their soul and make sure I'm hiring a good person with a high level of integrity.

4. You must like the person you're interviewing. I know it's hard to interview someone and get a feel for who they really are. But listen to your gut. The bottom line is that your employees will be spending more time with you day-to-day than your family. You have to like the person you're hiring. I always ask myself during the interview process whether I would enjoy having a beer or a cup of coffee with the person I'm interviewing. If I answer yes, then there's a good chance I would hire that person.

5. Sometimes a potential quality employee is hard to pass up, even if you don't have a current position available. There were numerous times I interviewed someone I really liked, but I didn't have a position for them. Good employees are hard to come by. If you interview a potential superstar employee, hire that person, regardless if there's a position available. Chances are, you'll find the right position in your company for your superstar employee in due time.

Compensation plan

When it comes to paying your employees, pay them fair market value based on the position. The comp plan that was success-ful for me was paying my employees a salary plus commission plus bonus. The salary was a bit below market value, but the commission compensated for the lower salary. My strategy to pay salary plus commission was based on the fact that I wanted my employees to have skin in the game. The more successful the business was (based on sales), the more my employees would make. I also wanted employees to feel that they were part of the success and would be compensated for helping to grow the company. By the same token, if you take a portion of their salary and convert it to commission, and the business experiences an economic downturn or business is down, you aren't obligated to pay higher salaries. You're only on the hook for the salary you guaranteed.

Bonuses are based on outperformance. We worked off budgets and forecasts. If we outperformed our budget in excess of ten percent then my employees were eligible for a bonus. The more money the business owners make, the more money their employees should make.

Career advancement

The first thing I told my employees once they were hired is that I have a commitment to them as my employee. I told them it was my responsibility as their leader to make sure they were better off financially, emotionally, and professionally a year from the day they started working for me. I backed that up by having a philosophy of promoting from within. Whenever there was an open position, it was always first open to internal employees before I looked outside the company. This practice created a real opportunity for employees' career growth and gave them the ability to make more money. This practice is a benefit to any business owner, because it promotes career growth and decreases turnover. And let's face it, turnover and training are very expensive. Having long-term employees is a good recipe for consistency in a company.

Mentoring and training

It's your responsibility as the business owner to mentor your employees. You want to set them up for success, and there are a few ways to accomplish that goal. Push them as hard as you can but know their limits. Continue to train them and take their input about the business seriously. Offer training in other areas of your company, so they can be cross-trained in different aspects of the business.

As the owner, have an open-door policy. Make your office a safe place to come if they want to discuss an issue. However, realize that there's a hierarchy in your business. Don't step on any of your managers' toes. Never talk salary increases with employees who aren't your direct reports. Leave it up to your managers to make salary decisions. Build rapport with all of your employees. It's imperative that you have a good pulse on your company and you do everything in your power not to be blindsided.

Lead by example. Never put yourself in any compromising position that can do harm to your company. Always remember, you might love your employees but know that, under any circumstance, you love your company more. Never let employees think they are bigger than your company. When they do, it causes trouble. Don't be shy – let them know this attitude isn't acceptable.

Company spirit

You must be the biggest cheerleader for your company. Praise your employees when warranted as well as holding your employees accountable. Be vigilant about employee performance reviews. You never want to blindside employees. They should know where they stand in regard to their job performance. Keep in mind that you need to provide a comfortable work environment and, by the same token, make sure they're enjoying what they're doing. Build camaraderie. Once a year host a company-sponsored event that promotes team building. If everyone works as a team, you'll be successful.

These are just some of the tips I recommend to help build a great company culture. Remember, a great culture leads to a great company.

Chapter 6

Growing pains

Within two years, all the building efforts I put into Acrobat Outsourcing really started paying off. In the second year, our revenue more than doubled. But it wasn't without challenges and growing pains.

After Johnny Diego had become my right-hand man, I found out he was charging employees for the best jobs such as being a concessionaire at the San Francisco Giants games. Johnny was "selling" that job, telling employees they had to give him $5 if they wanted the opportunity to sell hotdogs and beer at the games. I had no idea this was going on or how long he had been doing it. I only found out when an employee mentioned to me that he really wanted to work the upcoming Giants game, but he didn't have $5 to give to Johnny.

"Five bucks?" I said, "What are you talking about?"

"Yeah, that's what he charges."

When I called Johnny into my office and confronted

him, he started talking in circles. It pained me to do it, but I fired him. I couldn't have that underhanded activity going on in my business. Johnny understood – he thanked me for giving him the opportunity of working at Acrobat and for being his mentor. He said he felt terrible that he let me down.

He had been the epitome of an employee. I always told every one of my employees: I love you, but I love my business more. If you think you're bigger than Acrobat, we're going to have issues. Johnny thought he was bigger than Acrobat, and he got stung for having that attitude, because I can't run a company like that.

During the hospital strike, I hired a bookkeeper I really liked. She seemed to know what she was doing. She'd come in once a week to pick up all the accounts payable. I'd go to her house to go over numbers, and I met her husband. She always had good news, and I was always happy with the numbers. She told me everything I wanted to hear.

Then one day I got a letter from the IRS stating I was facing fines for not paying my payroll taxes. I called the bookkeeper and asked what she knew about this. She was supposed to be paying the taxes. But she was all over the board – saying of course she paid the taxes, but she'd have to look into it. I asked my accountant to look over everything. Due to sloppy bookkeeping practices, my bookkeeper hadn't paid the payroll taxes for two quarters in a row.

This happened right in the middle of a huge growth spurt for Acrobat, and I thought it would end us. I was using every dime I made to fund the growth, so an unexpected bill for over $60,000 was devastating. Here's how I operated at the time: As long as I had money to make payroll for my internal employees and hundreds of temp employees, I was good. But I didn't have any money in reserve. Where was I going to come up with $60,000? I was panicked and furious.

I was so mad I hired an attorney, intending to sue my bookkeeper. But I had so much going on at the time. I was able to work out a payment plan with the IRS and avoid penalties for the unpaid taxes, so my business didn't get into trouble. My business was really growing, so I eventually decided to drop the case. The bookkeeper was so happy when I dropped the case that she sent a huge bouquet of flowers to the office. It didn't make me feel better! I just looked at the situation as one of the trials and tribulations that go with owning your own business. But from that day forward, I checked every week to make sure the payroll taxes were paid. I hired another bookkeeper, who stayed with Acrobat for years until we were so big I had to hire an entire finance department.

I lost my father to lung cancer around this time, which made everything harder. My dad was a simple guy who wore jeans to work every day. But he worked hard and taught me about work ethic. He was such a generous, genuine man. If his neighbor won the lottery, my father wouldn't be envious. He'd be truly happy for his neighbor. And you know someone's legacy by their funeral. When my dad passed, there must've been 300 people at our temple. A police brigade led us to the cemetery.

Dad was an amazing guy. But he made some mistakes too. He had an affair, and my parents ended up getting divorced after being married for twenty-five years. I'll never forget that, when he was on his deathbed, he apologized to my brother and me. He said he was sorry for what he'd done to our mom and to our family and that it was the worst mistake of his life.

Then he said, "Steve, I know you're not in a great marriage, and you're not very happy. Don't do what I did. If you're going to leave your marriage, do it the right way. Leave it."

I remembered his advice later when my first marriage ended. I couldn't talk to my father about business strategy, but he taught me a lot about life. And he was my biggest fan. I just wish he could have lived long enough to see how much I was able to accomplish with Acrobat.

I always regarded my dad as my hero. And, as an entrepreneur, I think it's important to have a business mentor. I met my mentor, Bob, prior to acquiring Acrobat. He was a successful businessman and overall amazing human being. He taught me so much, and I trusted him implicitly. I held onto every word this guy said. I talked to him every single day about business and philosophy. Sometimes he'd give me tough love. Sometimes he would give me accolades. And I loved Bob and his wife. Bob was my guy, especially after my dad passed.

When I first started Acrobat, having my mentor by my side gave me peace of mind, because I had someone I could go to for advice, direction, and support. Bob guided me and really helped me start and grow my business. At first, he was right by my side. He would ask all the time, "What can I do for you?"

As the business started to grow, Bob wanted to be compensated for his help. At first he said, "Pay me $5,000 a month as a consultant, and you'll have access to me whenever you want." He was working a regular full-time job at that time. I agreed to the deal, because he was a valuable asset. However, things started to change.

Bob lived in Sacramento. When I opened my Sacramento office, he helped me staff it with people he knew. He brought in my first Sacramento salesperson and helped to hire my first Sacramento operations manager. At first, this was great. But it created a situation in which they were loyal to Bob, not necessarily loyal to me or Acrobat. If I asked them to do something, they might or might not do it. But if Bob asked them, they were all over it! This wasn't ideal, but I thought Bob had my best interests at heart.

Despite the fact he was working a full-time job elsewhere, Bob asked me to lease a car for him. Again, he was my guy. I agreed and leased a car through our business, a beautiful new Acura MDX. Then he started trying to get more involved in my business. He was trying to run things the way he wanted to run them. I had known Bob for six years; this was the first time I started feeling like he was taking advantage of me and my business. Bob was a well-known player in the foodservice space. He had promised to bring in all this new business that never came to fruition. I started losing control over the employees in Sacramento, because they were taking direction from Bob, not from me. And it created a power struggle.

Then, when the economy started heading for trouble later that year and my social-events business started dropping. I had to go into survival mode and make cuts. I remember telling Bob that I couldn't afford to pay him $5,000 a month anymore. I asked him to take a pay cut down to $2,000 a month for a while, which insulted him. Three months later, business was still dropping, and I had to watch every penny. But Bob never stuck his neck out. Not once, when business started drying up and I was struggling to make payroll, did Bob offer to take a pay cut. It rubbed me the wrong way. Eventually, I had to cut his consulting fee down to $2,000 a month and, later, I cut it altogether. The relationship soured completely. I continued to pay his car payment to fulfill the three-year lease. But I stopped talking to Bob.

Looking back, I'll always cherish everything he did for me in the early days of owning my business. I learned a lot from Bob including many of my philosophies about how to run a business. I think that Bob had always been the teacher, and I had always been the student. After buying Acrobat and gaining so much business experience, I was no longer the student. We were on the same level. That changed our relationship, and it also made me realize I didn't need to lean on Bob as if he were a crutch.

After Bob and I parted ways, I had to do a whole sweep of the Sacramento office. Even though he was only a consultant, the employees he brought to Acrobat were regularly meeting with him and probably reporting everything we were doing in that office. I needed a clean slate.

The poor economy was dictating my business. I had no control over the recession. Good customers and good business started getting more difficult to come by. I started noticing that caterers were no longer calling for temp employees. All my server business was drying up. Country clubs didn't need any more temp staff. I went into panic mode. My business was taking a serious hit, but we kept marketing anyway. That's when I got the call from the "little" company in Cupertino called Apple. Apple was self-running its employee cafeterias. An Apple manager called and asked if I had any temps I could send over. Of course we did, and we soon became Apple's exclusive provider of temporary staffing services. This started a business relationship that would both save Acrobat and almost kill it.

Chapter 7

The economic storm

As an entrepreneur, you will face times in business when you have to make sacrifices. We were in the midst of a severe economic downturn, and it was a time of sacrifice. But I didn't know that at first.

Apple continued to grow into a major account for Acrobat Outsourcing. Right before business got really slow, I decided to open an office in San Diego. I wanted to expand beyond the Bay Area, and I knew San Diego would be a viable market for staffing services. This market had everything I needed. There was plenty of corporate business – company headquarters, hospitals, hotels, and country clubs – and it fit all of our criteria. The economy was going south, my social-events business was nonexistent, and I was leaning on my corporate business. Because I had Apple, I was able to fund a new market. I took a risk, and I opened a new office in San Diego in a down market. I hired two women to run that office – one in sales, one in recruiting – and we had big plans for San Diego.

However, this market didn't take off the way I hoped it would. I figured I just needed to get the machine going, but it wasn't happening. Unfortunately, the people I hired weren't the ideal employees to open a new market in a bad economy. They were both kind and sweet, and they fit the Acrobat culture. But in this situation, I needed rainmakers – people who could take the market by storm, really get their arms around it, and own it as if it was their own business. People who would build it and grow it. There was business in San Diego, and I thought it would be a great fit. But after nine months, I realized we didn't have the momentum we needed. I had earned very little revenue to offset the investment, and I had to take a hard look at San Diego.

My social-events business was dying in the rest of my offices, and I couldn't afford to carry an office that wasn't making any money. Unfortunately, I had to make the difficult decision to close the new office. Here's the lesson I learned from that experience: You have to hire the right people for the culture and the right people for the situation. I needed employees who had the passion to succeed, no matter what.

Closing the San Diego office, however, wasn't enough to keep me out of trouble during the recession. I'll never forget looking at my profit and loss (P&L) statement in August and seeing that it was down a quarter of a million dollars for the first half of the year. That's when panic struck. I had to get my arms around this business because, if I didn't, I would be closing up shop. By that point, I'd spent way too much time, money, and effort getting my business going. If I wanted to keep it going, I had to stop the bleeding.

The last thing I wanted to cut was internal staff. If there was anything we didn't need, then we didn't spend money on it. I reviewed every expense and every vendor from background-check companies, to HR consultants, to IT consultants. For every single expense, I asked, "Is this a must-have for my business or a nice-to-have?" Any nice-to-haves got cut. I cut every luxury I could out of my business, because now we were working on a shoestring budget. And all expenses had to be approved. I felt that if we could keep everything lean and mean, then we could power through the recession. I even questioned the need for paperclips!

The only thing I did not cut was my marketing efforts. The money I saved by closing San Diego, I spent on marketing. I knew the economy would eventually come back. Even though I stopped seeing marketing campaigns from all my competitors, I kept spending money on that line item. Business kept disappearing, but I had a gut feeling our marketing efforts would pay off in the long run.

In the meantime, as business disappeared, I was left with two accounts making up over seventy percent of my total revenue – Apple and Stanford University.

I didn't love the Stanford account, because I didn't see eye-to-eye with the manager there. The school started working with us a few years earlier, and we provided temporary server staff for its graduation events, faculty parties, and special events. For one event, early in the relationship, the manager ordered thirty servers. He required that I come with the staff ahead of time, so he could check in the employees. This was a strange request, but I showed up with my temp employees. The Stanford manager lined up my temps, and then went down the line, rejecting half of them based solely on their looks. They weren't young enough or attractive enough or whatever he was looking for.

Finally, I said, "Okay. Enough." This was not how I conducted business. These employees had come here expecting to work, and just because he didn't like the way they looked, he expected me to send them home with no pay.

"I'm not going to do that," I said. "Either you take them all – and they all work – or I take them all with me."

That insulted him, but I had to force his hand. He took all my employees, because it was too late to get another staffing company. Now, I was very happy to be working with Stanford – it was a high-profile client that regularly used our services. But I didn't like working with this guy from the beginning. And despite all the extra trouble, I couldn't let go of a bad customer, because I needed that revenue.

Our other main account, Apple, just kept getting bigger and bigger. That account kept me afloat. This was a great, high-profile account I could lean on, feel good about, and even use as a marketing tool to get more business. But as much as I needed and loved getting Apple's business, I was also getting nervous, because this one account made up so much of my overall revenue.

If Apple went away, I would lose millions of dollars in revenue. I would practically have to start my business from scratch. Accounts come and go, and you have to be ready for that. I knew I was in a risky position. You have to be prepared for the fact that some customers may not renew their contract with you and may stop using your services. Temporary staffing is such a reactionary business that you can lose a big customer in one day. That's why it's important to stay in touch with your customer base, so you always know where you stand with them. And if there's a problem, you need to react immediately and take care of the situation. Communication is an integral part of success.

I knew if I lost one account – Apple or Stanford – I could be out of business. That could be the nail in the coffin. My dependence on these accounts made me nervous and, it turned out, it made my bank nervous. I had a $1 million credit line with my bank, and I was relying on that credit line to fund my payroll and grow my business.

One day, I was in my San Jose office, and I got a call from a bank representative. She wanted to interview me, so the bank could better understand my business. She came into the office and sat down with me. We talked about the business, and I shared the financials with her. They weren't great, by the way, because of the economy. When I showed her the P&L,

she noticed that two accounts made up the majority of business. This made the bank a little wary, she said. At some point in the conversation – I'm not even sure how it came up – I mentioned I was going through a divorce. This made her even more nervous.

A week later, I received a notice from my bank saying that my business was too high risk, and it was cutting off my line of credit. The bank managers weren't comfortable continuing to give me money, because they weren't sure my business was a good investment. I was distraught. I had sixty days to find a new bank to help me finance my company. And I needed financing, because I had a huge monster of an account (Apple) sucking my bank account dry – that account kept growing and I needed to ensure my payroll expenses didn't outpace accounts receivable.

I was worried. But I had learned throughout my career that I couldn't let my employees see me sweat. When your employees see you sweat, they get nervous. And when they get nervous, things start to unravel. They lose focus on the business at hand. It's human nature to want to protect yourself and your income. People will do whatever they can to survive. If they see the owner sweat, it affects the overall culture of your company. It affects employee productivity. Employees start looking for other jobs, and they stop putting all their energy into their work. I couldn't let anyone see how nervous I was.

I remember sitting at my desk, worrying about the situation and asking myself, "What have I done?" I put five years of blood, sweat, and tears into this business, and I was not about to give up now. I had sacrificed so much. I was separated from my wife. I had two young kids and I had a huge financial responsibility to my family. I had no choice but to make Acrobat work.

So I scrambled and called every business bank to see if they would give me any kind of financing. All I could find was Wells Fargo – and it wouldn't be an ideal situation. They offered their factoring program: Wells Fargo would buy eighty percent of my receivables and charge me a very high interest rate in return. I had been paying a minimal interest rate at my previous bank. With Wells Fargo, the interest rate was so high it would negatively impact my P&L. For example, if I borrowed $100,000 from my previous bank, I'd pay back about $104,000. With Wells Fargo, I'd pay back $112,000. This would have a direct impact on my bottom line. But I had no choice, because I needed the financing to keep this business going.

Every week, I had to send Wells Fargo my receivables. All the money I was making went to Wells to fund my payroll and expenses. I knew this relationship with Wells Fargo was not a long-term solution; it was more like a Band-Aid that I put into place until I could establish a relationship with another bank.

This was not an easy time to get money. And based on our bank statements, P&L statements, and customer lists, my company didn't look that great on paper. Banks love customers that don't have a high concentration of business coming from any single customer account. They love customers that have an aging report of thirty days or less. My aging report was about sixty-five days, because Apple was such a big portion of my business and it had the power to dictate payment terms that worked in its favor. Plus, the banks I met with noticed the customers I had in prior years weren't doing business with us anymore, because the economy was not in great shape. To a bank, we were a high-risk client.

I was stuck. But, once again, I go back to one of my favorite sayings: "Persistence overcomes resistance." I persevered and kept looking. When I found a bank in Silicon Valley called Bridge Bank that specialized in providing funding for small businesses, it was almost like a gift from God.

I remember meeting with these folks, and they loved my business. They came to the rescue and paid off my Wells Fargo debt, so I was no longer at its mercy. Bridge gave me more money than I needed, so I had a cushion to lean on.

Scrambling for money and being so close to losing everything kept me up at night and made me feel queasy almost every day. But as an entrepreneur, you're a risk taker. You've got to have a strong stomach, and you've got to really believe in yourself and your company. You've got to believe everything will work out. After three years of hard times, the economy started improving. And my marketing efforts began paying off. Little by little, my previous customers started coming back, and I started getting new customers.

The recession was a great learning experience. I believe that, as an entrepreneur, being in dark places and figuring out how to pull yourself out will make you stronger. I had so many things going against me that I could've easily closed my doors. Many of my competitors did. But looking back, sacrificing was one of the best decisions I made. Cutting costs and putting that money into marketing set us up for future growth. The only employees I lost during this economic downturn were the two employees in San Diego when I closed that office. Otherwise, we all weathered the storm. And, just like I knew it would, Acrobat recovered.

Chapter 8

Losing $7 million in one day

Six years after buying Acrobat Outsourcing, the economy began to recover, and I started to see a shift in our business. We were getting calls from new customers. Revenue started growing. We started getting busy again. We were no longer relying on a few customers. And we became a force to be reckoned with.

When the economy began turning around, my marketing investment began to pay off exactly the way I'd hoped and predicted it would. All was good at Acrobat. The Apple account was growing and thriving. The social-events business was coming back. I'd taken market share away from small competitors that went out of business during the economic recession. Before the recession, we were merely a thorn in the side of our largest competitor. We emerged from the recession as a formidable competitor.

I always lived my life with the motto "low risk, low reward/high risk, high reward." That defines a key trait of being an entrepreneur. Another entrepreneurial trait I have is the fact that I'm never satisfied. Because of that, I always wanted more. I had a vision of taking Acrobat nationwide and, although I failed at trying to open a San Diego office, I wasn't about to give up now. My mind and my spirit were in expansion mode. The timing was right, and I had the revenue from Apple to help fund that expansion.

At first, I was torn on how I wanted to expand. I could either do it via acquisition or organically by establishing a new office. If I expanded via acquisition, I would have instant market share and revenue coming in from day one. The problem with an acquisition is making sure the company you acquire shares the same values and culture as your company. If there's a disconnect, it can turn out to be a disaster. If it's done right, it could turn out to be a great investment. I decided to try both strategies: Purchase an office via acquisition and open a new San Diego office.

I learned about a small company in Los Angeles called Up To Par Staffing, which exclusively provided temporary staff to golf courses and country clubs. The company was for sale, because the owner was relocating to manage an exclusive country club. I knew I wanted to be in L.A., and I knew if I did it organically, it would take a long time to establish Acrobat in a market with so much competition. After much thought and due diligence, I decided to pursue Up To Par Staffing. Knowing the former owner had just received a job offer he couldn't turn down, I had a bit of leverage to negotiate a deal. After a few weeks of negotiating, we finally agreed. Up To Par Staffing in L.A. was my first acquisition.

The business operated out of a tiny office. The two internal employees handled both staffing and recruiting. The employees, like anyone would be in that situation, were uncomfortable when I took over the business. They may have been afraid they'd lose their jobs. I met with them and told them about our company, told them about our culture, and assured them that they were an important part of the equation and the team. I wasn't firing them. I was going to lean on them and empower them to help me grow the L.A. business. I told them I acquired the business, because I saw a tremendous opportunity in L.A. We would be able to take their current book of business and expand it rapidly.

I explained that our culture and compensation plan are based on being totally transparent and making every Acrobat employee part of the success. I explained that we shared our financials on a monthly basis, and our internal employees always knew where they stood. This model was successful with my other offices, because it got everyone involved, rewarded everyone for filling temp jobs, and the more jobs we filled, the more money everyone makes. Within a short time, these two new employees were on board and thriving, and Acrobat's L.A. operation was moving ahead.

Next, I turned my attention to San Diego. I learned so much the first time I opened an office in

San Diego, and I was determined not to make the same mistake twice. This time I was more methodical in my approach.

First, I identified a good location for a new office. I wanted it to be centrally located, have good access to public transportation, and be a place where my employees and I would be proud to come, without breaking the bank.

Second, I hired a salesperson. I was very particular about the qualities I needed to make this expansion work. I needed a rainmaker who was not afraid of rejection, believed in my vision and culture, and would overturn every rock to find business.

Third, I needed a staffing manager who would work tirelessly to staff jobs. To fill that role, I transferred my assistant staffing manager from San Francisco. She was very familiar with the Acrobat business model and culture. San Diego was now open for business.

Solidifying a few more preferred vendor agreements that year helped to get those new locations going. One of our big customer agreements was with Aramark, a large foodservice company that manages cafeterias and cafes in colleges, corporations, hospitals, and stadiums. This is a huge company, and getting this agreement was a feather in our cap. By getting preferred vendor status, we were really getting a "hunting license" to sell staffing services everywhere Aramark operated. Aramark gave us preferred status to all of its accounts throughout the United States. This was a defining moment for Acrobat

Outsourcing, and this opportunity enabled us to grow our business in our existing locations and nationwide.

Now, six years after I purchased Acrobat, my company had arrived. We were the preferred vendor for multiple customers. Plus, my concession business and my professional sports team business started kicking in. I started doing business with the Oakland A's, Oakland Raiders, and San Jose Sharks. We provided staff for every concert venue in the Bay Area. Things were good. But the fact that I still had a lot of concentration on Apple gnawed at me.

In the midst of all this growth and opportunity, however, I started noticing that my company was broken. At the time, San Francisco (my corporate headquarters) was bringing in eighty percent of the overall revenue. But when I looked around that office, morale was not good. People weren't filling jobs like they used to; they weren't calling customers back. They were taking the path of least resistance and just looking for a paycheck. There was infighting; I had people in my office complaining about other employees. Leadership below me showed favoritism. There was no accountability. Our business hours were 6:00 in the morning until 9:00 at night. All the employees started leaving at 6:00 p.m., and if you called the office after that, no one answered the phone. I started getting complaints from customers. I started seeing poor evaluations of our temp staff. I didn't like the energy that was going on in that office.

One day, the senior operations manager, a staffing manager, and another employee in my San Francisco office asked for a private meeting. I have an open-door policy so, of course, I said yes. They told me the staffing manager in charge of a key account was acting erratic.

This employee was a superstar who practically worked around the clock to grow this key account. My first reaction was, "That's impossible." I probably talked with her thirty times a day and never saw the slightest sign of erratic behavior. But these three told me they saw her sniffing a lot and her behavior was becoming unpredictable. I thought, well, I could have missed something. Although I thought highly of this particular employee and she was such an integral part of my company, I owed it to my team to investigate the claims. (I always say that I love my employees, but I love my business more.)

I didn't want to confront her, because you can't accuse someone without evidence. So I conducted an internal investigation and talked with several other employees in the office. When I started talking with other people, I learned that my senior operations manager – one of the three who made the accusation – was cultivating a clique within the company. The three women who made the accusation were friends. If you weren't part of their clique, they made life miserable for you. And they were gunning for this employee. There was jealousy, there was animosity, and they just wanted her out. In the end, I realized they invented the story about erratic behavior and the implication of possible drug use. They were trying to get her fired.

These three employees thought they were bigger than Acrobat. They thought they could spread rumors about a coworker, and they thought I would side with them. I knew I needed to protect the Acrobat culture. As I dug into this issue, I learned the problem wasn't just infighting and false accusations. There was more.

The "life expectancy" of a staffing manager is about two years before they start burning out. When you're staffing jobs, the temp employees don't consider this work as their number-one priority, so you deal with a lot of disappointment when employees call and cancel at the last minute or when they don't represent Acrobat well. It's thankless, because you spend most of your time fielding calls and putting out fires. Very rarely do you get, "Oh, you guys did such a great job. Thank you so much for staffing our event." Why? Because the customer expects you'll do a great job.

When you hear complaints over and over again and you're constantly trying to find temp employees to staff jobs, you start burning out and taking the path of least resistance. Instead of calling the list of great employees to get that job filled, you just schedule whoever's available. Some people are always available for a reason – they can't keep a steady job. These are the people who can't hold it together. Then the customer calls and complains. If you no longer care about what you're doing and you don't take time to put the right people into the job, it kills the company's reputation.

And that's what was happening to Acrobat. Our quality was suffering, and our reputation was suffering.

I couldn't just turn my back on that. I had to make a difficult decision and let go of my San Francisco staffing manager and my senior operations manager. I knew this could have a devastating effect on my San Francisco business, but it had to be done, because I could not allow that kind of behavior to continue. Again, culture is such an important aspect of a company's success, and you have to be relentless to maintain it. If you let the culture slip, it can be detrimental in the long run. I was not going to let that happen to my company.

With two key employees gone, I had to roll up my sleeves, get in the weeds, and get Acrobat back where I wanted it. Now that I was back in the trenches, I discovered we had been understaffing customer job requests to the point that I had to fight to keep multiple accounts. Companies were disappointed in our poor service, and I had to convince them I would meet their staffing needs even though we hadn't met their needs in the past.

I took over both critical operations – staffing and recruiting – and I had to take a lot of lemons and turn them into lemonade. I went from driving the company vision to being involved in day-to-day operations, trying to save my company. But the effort paid off. These changes helped Acrobat transition into the leading staffing company it is today.

During that time, I hired two monumental employees. The first was Paul Rickett, who came to Acrobat after spending years in federal prison. He had been in the U.S. Army and, when he left, he started using drugs. His addiction took over his life to the point where his family had disowned him. He was living in his car and, to fund his drug habit, he started counterfeiting money. He'd counterfeit a $20 bill and sell it for $10. He was counterfeiting thousands of dollars a week. Eventually, federal agents nabbed him, and he spent a few years in prison. When he got out, he went to a halfway house for newly released federal inmates. That brought him to Acrobat, looking for a job.

When I interviewed Paul, it was obvious he was smart. Before getting involved in drugs, he had been the director of IT for a major hospital. He was looking for a second chance, and I believe in second chances.

We had Paul start as a server working events in San Francisco. He appreciated the job, and in a short time he became one of our top servers. We put him in charge of the server training program for Acrobat Academy, so he was teaching people how to serve and helping them get better positions. Paul loved the work he was doing for us. He worked both of the Steve Jobs memorial services. One was a quiet and somber event where he served dignitaries and high-profile people such as Bill and Hillary Clinton, Bill Gates, and Condoleezza Rice. The second memorial was held at Apple, where they had a huge party headlined by Coldplay. Paul was the top server there, serving celebrities and musicians. It was such an eye-opening experience for him. Not that long ago, he had been sitting behind bars. Paul really embraced this opportunity.

I promoted Paul to be a staffing manager at Acrobat, and he went from making $12 an hour to $50,000 a year with benefits. I gave him the responsibility of staffing all of San Francisco's jobs. He embraced that too. From there, he became my top-selling staffing manager. He worked twelve to fourteen hours a day, sometimes sixteen hours a day. Putting Paul in that position helped change my San Francisco office from broken to, not only fixed, but proud and gaining momentum. Today, Paul is Acrobat's director of client services. He married a wonderful woman and saved enough money to buy a house. He's definitely living happily ever after. I'm so proud of Paul.

The other key employee I hired was a salesperson. When I decided to take the plunge and reopen an office in San Diego, I knew I needed a rainmaker. I needed an assassin to go out and get business. I came across a salesman named Marc Caplan. Marc had worked for Walt Disney and Aramark, and he had sold point-of-sale systems to restaurants. He was energetic and the nicest guy you'd ever want to meet. He believed in my vision, he wanted to work for Acrobat, and I wanted to hire him.

I sent Marc an offer package. Back then, no one negotiated. But he wanted to negotiate, and he wanted to negotiate hard. And, I have to tell you, I respected it. Now, I didn't really agree to what he was asking, but I remember thinking, "Boy, if this guy is willing to negotiate this hard, that's a guy I want on my team." I negotiated with Marc more than I had with anyone else, because I wanted him to work for me. He had the skillset, and I knew he fit our culture. He was very green when it came to industry knowledge, so I would be able to mold him to become a successful salesperson within my company.

Marc was in charge of southern California. This time, we embraced San Diego. Thanks to Marc, we were generating revenue in a very short time. He also generated additional revenue for L.A., making that a viable market. After my recent experience with difficult employees, Marc was a breath of fresh air. He was entrepreneurial, and he bought into my vision of what I wanted this company to look like. Marc became my protégé in a way that reminded me of my relationship with Bob. Marc became a tremendous asset for Acrobat.

Now, six years after buying Acrobat, we were having an amazing year. We were on track to double our revenue from the year before. But that all changed when I got the phone call that I hoped I'd never get on all my sleepless nights. That phone call came from Apple.

Apple made an internal change to its procurement department by bringing in a young, hotshot guy who wanted to make a difference. He was committed to making a splash. And it turned out Acrobat was his first splash.

He called one day and asked me to come to his office. I knew something was up, but I didn't know what. I drove to Apple, and I walked into the office. Let me tell you, I did not like this guy from the get-go. I could tell he had an agenda. During the meeting, we sat down in the Apple café, and he said, "Steve, we're going to terminate our contract with Acrobat. We just need to get a bigger company in here."

He tried to make it sound like everything was going to be great – Apple would transition us out over a few months, so I wasn't losing the entire account in one day. He wanted the transition to be smooth, he wanted us to work closely with the new company, and he wanted to thank me for all our service over the years. He ended it by saying he wished me nothing but the best of luck.

My first reaction was shock. I was taught that if you lose a piece of business, you do it gracefully. Never burn bridges, because you don't know what the future might look like. I leaned on my personal philosophy: "Make every experience a positive experience." I was calm, and I promised we'd do whatever it took to make the transition smooth. But in my head, I knew I just lost everything I had rebuilt. We had survived the recession, loss of funding, and a major staffing overhaul. And now I lost my biggest account: $7 million in annual revenue.

After that meeting, I sat in my car in Apple's parking lot thinking, "Holy crap, what just happened? How am I ever going to overcome this obstacle? Am I going to have to lay off my staff? Am I going to have to close the new offices?" I remember going back to the office, thinking of every possible way I could replace the Apple business. I didn't want to lay off anyone, so the first thing I did was cut my own salary and distributions.

The second thing I did was get my team together to brainstorm potential ways to grow the business. I brought together a task committee with my marketing manager, my new employees, and my salespeople. I knew I couldn't let them see me sweat, so I didn't tell them we were losing Apple. We sat down in a room with a whiteboard in a discreet location, and I said, "All right. A new year is coming up. Let's brainstorm ways to grow the business moving forward."

I believe the more income streams you have, the better off you are. We came up with two ideas. The first was promoting our staffing services to restaurants. Acrobat had never provided temp staffing to restaurants, because most couldn't afford our services. Their margins are very slim. Corporate cafeterias and catering companies could afford us, because they passed the cost back to their customers. With restaurants, they can't pass that cost back to their customers, because that's not how their business model works. But we thought if we could start marketing and penetrating the restaurant business, we could drive revenue.

So we started marketing temp staffing to restaurants as Culinary Outsource Services. We started calling virtually every restaurant in San Francisco and

L.A. to see if, in fact, we could get temp staffing in those establishments.

The other piece of our Culinary Outsource Services program was offering an undercover customer. Our trained employee would go into a restaurant, critique the entire operation, and then give a report to the restaurant owner. (This was before online review platforms became widespread.) We went like gangbusters on marketing. We had a couple of bites on that program, but it never got off the ground. We did, however, have moderate success getting restaurants to use our temp staffing services.

The other vertical we created was convention staffing. We put together a presentation and went into big convention centers and visitor bureaus in San Francisco, L.A., Sacramento, San Jose, and San Diego, offering staff for conventions. That was an automatic, instant revenue stream. All those cities have convention centers where national organizations meet. These large events require hundreds of employees to stuff bags, register guests, set up for events, and break down after events. Plus, they hold smaller conventions for state-level organizations. These events take place in hotels rather than large convention centers, happen more frequently, and are less labor intensive than the bigger events. So this new initiative helped us recoup that lost revenue.

We got back on course. I hired the right people. And even after losing Apple, that business was replaced with everything else we had going on. We had to readjust, but by having the right team in place – and the resourcefulness to find new business – it worked.

Chapter 9

Coast-to-coast expansion

Now, seven years after buying Acrobat – and after losing the Apple contract – we got a couple of big breaks that allowed us to grow beyond California and go national. This proved that sometimes a painful loss leads to greater gains.

The executive chef at Apple left and became the executive chef at Dropbox. At that time, Dropbox was a new company and was considered the new "unicorn" startup of Silicon Valley. Dropbox was well funded, and it used a portion of its venture capital to build a kitchen in its headquarters. The new executive chef at Dropbox put in place the same model he'd been using at Apple, and he brought in Acrobat Outsourcing to staff the kitchen.

The Dropbox headquarters was only a few blocks away from our office. So it was a perfect fit for both companies to work together. Also, from a strategic standpoint, working with Dropbox gave us clout that ultimately opened the door to many other accounts throughout San Francisco and the entire Bay Area. The relationship with Dropbox started with a few temp employees and grew into one of Acrobat's largest accounts.

That year, another former foodservice executive from Apple became chief culinary officer for Intel. He called us, because Intel was in the process of transitioning its kitchens to a self-run model instead of using a third party such as Sodexo or Aramark. Intel wanted to test this new model in its Austin, Texas, location. When Intel's chief culinary officer explained this to Marc (my VP of sales at the time), he asked, "Marc, are you interested in going to Austin?"

Because Marc is a sales guy who loves every deal, whether it's a good deal or not, he said, "Of course, I'd be interested."

Marc called me and explained what Intel wanted to do, and reminded me that we'd get Intel as a client right away. They would need fifteen, twenty, even thirty employees. I was interested in this opportunity, because Austin was like a smaller version of Silicon Valley. It has lots of corporate cafeterias. It has colleges and universities. It has hospitals, sports concessions, and so forth.

The only issue was that the margins with Intel wouldn't be as high as what we normally charged our clients for temporary staffing. They wanted a forty-five percent margin when our typical margin was closer to seventy percent. I hemmed and hawed about it, and I did some number crunching. When I took everything into consideration, it looked like we'd be a little better off than break even. This meant the office would be profitable right out of the gate, and we could start expanding throughout the city. I told Marc to go for it.

We met with the executive chef at Intel, and we won the request for proposal process. When all was said and done, Acrobat Outsourcing was now open for business in Texas, with Austin as the first of many offices we'd eventually have in that state. But opening an office in a new city, let alone a new state, comes with challenges.

First, we had absolutely no brand recognition and no pool of temp employees. Therefore, we couldn't lean on referrals from our temp employees to help us recruit new customer accounts.

Second, we weren't familiar with pay rates in Austin, so we had to be very careful about what to pay our temp employees. We could not afford to overpay, because the margins were so tight. On the other hand, we needed to pay our temp employees competitively, because it was our first entrance into a new market, and I was concerned about our reputation and making a good initial impression with our temp staff and customers. We needed quality people who wanted to work for Acrobat. And we needed to provide Intel with qualified employees, because that's how we sold the account, and that's what Intel expected.

We sent a task team to Austin to see what kind of employees we could recruit and to hire internal staff.

My task force was made up of people from my offices in California, so they understood the importance of hiring internal employees who aligned with our company culture and had a high level of commitment and entrepreneurial spirit. We needed to be very methodical in hiring the right people because, once again, it was important to set the right standard and expectations out of the gate. After numerous interviews and days of recruiting, we finally selected an all-star team.

From there, we needed to find an office that was centrally located and close to public transportation. We selected a location in Austin that was just a stone's throw away from Intel. Then we spent many weeks recruiting as many qualified temp employees as we could find. To help with our recruiting efforts, we also visited many colleges, veteran services organizations, and transitional housing units to cultivate relationships with these potential resources for employees.

We found out the Austin job market was pretty tight, but there were employees available when we looked. Like San Francisco, the city of Austin is dedicated to helping people who needed second chances find jobs. We were happy to oblige by giving these folks that chance. Some of these temp employees made the most of their opportunity, and some did not. However, at the end of the day, we provided the quality staff that Intel expected. We also secured some other accounts and had a roster of temp employees to fill those jobs. By the end of the year, Austin was open for business and poised for growth.

Even though we had lost the Apple account, which was devastating, it ended up being a blessing in disguise for us. This really was a transition year because, not only did we lose our biggest account, but we replaced it. We got to a point where we didn't have a heavy concentration on just one account. We were spreading our wealth, so to speak, to different accounts throughout our offices. Because of all that, we were strong enough to open Austin, our first market outside of California. Today, Austin is Acrobat's fourth or fifth largest market, and it all started with the Apple debacle.

Looking back, it was probably a great thing that the Apple account went away. It didn't feel that way when I first got the news, but it ended up working out in our favor. There's an old saying that goes something like, "When one door closes, another one opens." And that's exactly what happened.

Because of our strong growth, Acrobat was nominated for San Francisco's Small Business of the Year award. It was a huge honor for us, and the nomination underscored everything we had endured the previous years to get to this point. We had opened an office only to close it, weathered a recession, and lost our biggest account. But we remained resilient, and that was a huge reason why we received the nomination.

I remember attending the event with all the other nominees, where the mayor and board of supervisors would announce the winners. It was a fun night that only got better when they called Acrobat Outsourcing from the stage as the winner. I was so excited. I never thought we'd win, so I hadn't prepared a speech! But I got up in front of about 500 people and just started talking. To this day, I don't exactly remember what I said, but I remember attributing our success to the fact that we hired people nobody wanted to hire. I didn't care whether you were an ex-offender, a retired veteran, or someone with a disability. If you had the desire to work and a strong work ethic, that's what we cared about. That's what made Acrobat so successful. When I said this, the audience cheered and gave us a huge round of applause. In that moment, I realized how much good we were doing.

That year, we had overcome so many challenges, and we were recognized as San Francisco's Small Business of the Year. And we were giving people a second chance. The award was a huge honor that opened up a lot of doors. I started getting more exposure and more accounts. We were the Small Business of the Year, and we were growing into a *bigger* business.

Even though I was living in California and had no idea how it would ever happen, I always dreamed of having a business in New Jersey. I grew up there, so it would be like going home. This opportunity also arose that year.

My best friend from high school and I kept in touch over the years, and we often talked about what I was doing with Acrobat. He was really proud of how I built the business. One day he was talking about my business with one of his friends, a guy named Brian who just sold an employment agency. Brian was fascinated by what I'd built and with the business model, and he loved the idea of opening an Acrobat office in New Jersey.

Brian and I spoke, and we agreed he could open an office in New Jersey, duplicating my business model. I made a small investment as a partner and helped him set up the office, but he would keep the profits. I would get the additional exposure that went with opening an office on the other side of the country, and I'd get to fulfill my dream of having a business back home. Brian did all the initial groundwork, laid the foundation, followed my business model, hired internal people, built a roster of temp employees, and opened a New Jersey office.

He made a big splash for the opening. He invited the mayor of Woodbridge, where the office was located, and they held a ribbon-cutting ceremony. I remember flying out there and having childhood friends and family in the crowd. When I cut that ribbon, I nearly had tears in my eyes, because I couldn't believe I had pulled this off. I took a business that I started nearly 3,000 miles away and brought it to the area where I grew up. Standing there, among family, childhood friends, and New Jersey dignitaries and seeing everyone in the crowd, it felt like a gift from my father. I felt as though he helped make it all happen.

Unfortunately, things didn't work out as Brian planned. After a short time, he realized how much work it took to do temporary staffing. He didn't know if he had it in him to open a new business in a market with no brand recognition. And he and I didn't exactly see eye-to-eye on some things. I knew from experience that, when opening in new markets, you had to follow the business model. If you followed it, it would work. But he wanted to cut corners and change things. And he wasn't making any money. He was putting money into the business without getting anything back. Then he stopped paying the rent and really started struggling to keep the doors open.

He called one day and said, "Steve, I'm not sure I made the right decision by opening this office in New Jersey. I think I'm going to either close it or offer it to someone else."

Immediately I said, "You know what, I'll take it over. You can walk away." What else could I do? I wasn't going to close that office, and I wasn't going to let him sell it to someone. I was going to take it. When it came to my hometown, where my childhood friends and family were all watching, I was determined to make this work.

So Brian walked away. I took over the New Jersey office, and the first thing I had to do was find a new office, because we were getting evicted. I picked a place close to where my dad is buried. I know it sounds weird, but I thought he'd be watching over me and I'd be successful.

I brought in a childhood friend to run the office. She was looking for a job, and I needed someone I could trust. She was someone I could empower to treat it like her own business, follow the model, and get it going when I was on the opposite coast. And she did. First, business was slow and steady. But as we gained market share and got the machine running, New Jersey became a viable market for us.

I credit Brian for having the vision, foresight, and belief that Acrobat Outsourcing would flourish in New Jersey. I also believe this was meant to be. I was in the New Jersey office one day, and we were hiring people I had gone to high school with. It was a great feeling to be there, literally a quarter of a mile from my dad's final resting place and ten minutes from where I grew up. I believe in fate. Fate just took care of it. There may have been some bumpy roads along the way when we first started, but the New Jersey office has been thriving ever since.

Being able to replicate our California success in other markets gave me further confidence in our business model. It starts with *culture*. We are a team. We all work together, we've got everybody's back, we check in with each other, and we learn from each other. We hire people who fit the culture, and we use the same compensation plan throughout all our offices. We pay our internal people a base salary plus commission on the jobs they staff.

At its heart, every office is set up with two employees. One employee does the staffing; one employee does the recruiting. They work as a team, and they collaborate to recruit employees and to staff jobs. This basic model has to be supported by a salesperson, because we need both hunters and farmers. The staffing managers, my farmers, work with existing customers day-to-day, making sure their jobs are being staffed and looking for new opportunities with existing customers. The hunters are the salespeople who go out and get new business.

When you've got all three "machines" working at the same time, that's where the rubber meets the road. That's how we go to market. Over time, we discovered it has to be done this way because, otherwise, you get a void in gaining new customers or finding new temp employees or filling customers' jobs.

Due to our success in San Francisco, San Jose, Sacramento, and San Diego, we were able to duplicate this fundamental business model in both Austin and New Jersey. I truly believe that's what made us successful. That's how we gained traction in those markets. That's what created new revenue and new market share, practically right out of the gate.

Not everything I tried that year worked. After about nine months of marketing to restaurants under the name Culinary Outsource Services, I decided it was time to "cut bait." We were trying to get restaurants to use our services, but the margins were tight, and we weren't making much money. Plus, we discovered that restaurants are slow to pay their bills.

I also experimented with direct-placement strategies to find full-time employees for our customers. Unlike temporary staffing, companies use direct-placement services to help them find permanent employees. I started looking to acquire a direct-placement company that serves the hospitality industry. I found a boutique direct-placement foodservice company and bought it for $10,000. I hired the employee doing the direct-placement work as an internal employee for Acrobat. Her only responsibility was working with restaurants, hotels, and foodservice establishments on direct-placement opportunities. For example, if a restaurant was looking for an executive chef, the owner or manager would contact us, and we would find an executive chef that met their qualifications.

Our new Acrobat employee tried her hardest, and this new strategy worked for a little while. She got a couple of placements, but I think she started burning out. Also, our temporary staffing business was growing so fast and so dramatically that my direct-placement service wasn't really making an impact on our bottom line.

Since we had a lot of momentum and we were able to replace Apple's business with Dropbox and Intel, I saw that we were spinning our wheels on these new business efforts (Culinary Outsource Services and direct-placement services). But remember, these revenue streams came about because I lost Apple. So, in that crisis situation, I was throwing stuff against the wall to see what would stick. The more revenue streams you have coming into a company, the less vulnerable you are.

These initiatives just didn't work out, and when we recovered from the loss of the Apple business, we didn't really need them. I realized that getting rid of those underperforming programs would allow my internal salespeople to concentrate on the more profitable areas of our business, the "bread-and-butter" temporary staffing services that got us where we are today. Part of being an entrepreneur is making the decision to scrap what isn't working and concentrate on what you do best. For Acrobat Outsourcing, that's temporary staffing.

This was an important lesson for me – sometimes you have to look for new ideas, and sometimes you have to reassess and not be afraid to cut something that's not working. Part of owning your own business is accepting the fact that some things work and some things don't work. If it works, you continue to go with it. But if you realize an initiative doesn't work after you've invested time and money, then you have to know when to let go. Some entrepreneurs make the mistake of holding on too long, because they don't know "when to hold them and when to fold them." When you do make mistakes, don't dwell on them. Learn from them and move on.

On-target business advice

Growing your business: Acquisition versus organic growth

One critical decision most entrepreneurs need to make during the life cycle of their business is to figure out the right strategy to grow their business. The way I see it, you have two choices. Either duplicate your business model organically by expanding your breadth of business offerings or look for a target acquisition. Either way can be beneficial and prosperous. But you need to be aware that both strategies have their share of pros and cons. Let's first talk about organic growth.

Expanding your business via organic growth

One way to grow your business is to do it organically. This means bringing in additional goods or services that complement your current business offerings. Ultimately, you want to be able to offer your customers as much value as possible to keep them as a loyal customer. If you can become "the one-stop shop" to your customers and they rely on you for more than one service or product, then you're cultivating a meaningful relationship with your customers. This will make it hard for them to walk away from your business offerings.

When trying to grow your business organically, you need to keep in mind that, although there's an upfront investment, it's not close to what you'd be spending if you were to do an acquisition. Your risk is minimal, but there is much work to do on the front end. First, you need to determine if there is a market for the additional products or services you want to add to your current portfolio of business offerings. If so, you'll need to develop a pro forma (business plan) to determine if it makes sense to move forward. This will be your "playbook" to follow to reach your goals. Make sure you're as realistic as possible in the goals you're looking to achieve.

Next, earmark some funds for marketing. You need to get your name out there and start marketing your new product or service. Be strategic, have a clear picture of your target audience, and be very tactical on how to approach the market you're serving.

At the same time, create a buzz within your own company by getting your employees excited about the new business revenue stream. It's important to get buy-in from your employees, because you're relying on them to make this campaign successful. Offer an incentive to your employees to get this new product or service off the ground. Finally, take advantage of social media. Utilize as many resources as possible to get your name out there.

Once you complete your marketing plan, it's now time to move forward with the sales process. Start selling your product or service. Try selling to your existing customers first. It's much more cost effective to have existing customers buy your product or service than reaching out to new customers. You can also receive great feedback from existing customers, because of the relationships you've created. Offer an introductory promotion to accelerate sales during the launch of your new product or service.

Be relentless. Touch base with your customers periodically to keep your new product or service fresh in their minds. However, be aware that contacting your customers too often can backfire. Remember, there is a fine line between being assertive and being aggressive. Be aware of how you're coming across.

Finally, continue monitoring the success of your new product or service. Is it meeting or exceeding your expectations? This is a critical part of the process, because you should know within the first year or so whether the new product or service is on its way to profitability. If so, continue to ride the wave and keep marketing, selling, and delivering. If after a year or so you realize that it hasn't met your expectations and you're losing money, you might want to discontinue or adjust your new product or service. It's vital as an entrepreneur to know "when to hold them and when to fold them."

Expanding your business via acquisition

Another way to grow your business is via acquisition. Acquiring companies that complement your business model can be very rewarding. It gives an entrepreneur an instant revenue stream as well as an additional customer base to sell your other products or services. However, acquisition typically requires a large upfront investment. First, do your homework to find the right company to buy. Once you identify the company, make an initial offer you think the owner would accept.

Once your initial offer is accepted, you now enter the due diligence phase of the purchase. You now have the ability to really dissect the company you're buying. This is your one shot to look "under the hood" of a company and get a good feel for how the company performs financially, operationally, and culturally. I can't stress enough about how important it is to really understand the company you're about to buy. Most buyers concentrate on the financials and tend to overlook the intangibles. Will this company fit into your current company culture? What is the morale like? Is the leadership team equipped for growth? Do the leaders share the same vision as your company (the new parent company)? Do they have any customers that make up a high concentration of the overall business?

This is just a brief list of things to look for when acquiring a company. Your research also gives you a chance to renegotiate your initial offer based on what you learned about the company. (For more details on conducting due diligence, refer to the On-Target Business Advice section titled "How to conduct extensive due diligence prior to acquiring a company.")

Once the due diligence phase has been completed and you're moving forward with the acquisition, you need to be personally involved in the transition. Employees are nervous when they hear their company is being bought. It's up to you to be as transparent as possible for your new employees. It will pay dividends if they believe in your vision moving forward. By the same token, if you aren't disciplined in the due diligence cycle of the sale, you're taking a huge financial risk by buying a company that may not live up to your expectations. Furthermore, if the acquisition turns out to be a dud, you're out a great deal of money that will have a direct impact on your bottom line and your debt ratio.

Whichever route you pursue, do it with caution

When I'm ready to make a decision on business growth, I look at things three ways: What is the best-case scenario? What is the worst-case scenario? What is the most likely scenario? If I am at peace with each of these outcomes, I usually make the decision to proceed. But always with caution.

Chapter 10

Becoming salable

My top staffing manager was named Suzie. She owned the Apple account from its inception and grew it into a multimillion-dollar account. After we lost Apple and the executive chef from Apple went to Dropbox, it made sense for us to put Suzie on the Dropbox account. She did a great job; she worked well with Dropbox from the start, and she grew it into a flourishing account for Acrobat Outsourcing. But around this time, her coworkers in the San Francisco office started complaining about her, saying she was cocky and territorial and thought she knew it all. She started burning bridges with fellow employees, because she was aggressive and arrogant. And she stopped taking direction from her manager.

Suzie also became critical of Acrobat in general, complaining to me (the owner!) about how she wanted things done and criticizing just about everything. She also started making a lot of demands. Suzie and her husband were buying a house, and she wanted to work from home a couple of days a week. She wanted more money. And she was asking for more than I gave anyone else.

She became a difficult employee, and I needed to decide what to do about Suzie. On one hand, she had done a great job for me. She grew my business, and I owed her a lot for that. Dropbox absolutely adored her, loved working with her, and relied on her. From the customer's perspective, Suzie was a model employee. To my internal team in San Francisco, she was a nightmare coworker. The culture I'd cultivated was built on the idea of teamwork and that no one was better than anyone else. It was clear Suzie thought she was bigger than Acrobat. If I disregarded what my internal employees were telling me and didn't let her go, then it sent a message to everyone that some people mattered more than others.

Any time I had an employee who was not a team player, ran things their own way, talked down to other employees, made unreasonable demands, or showed disrespect to me, I made the tough decision without looking back. But with Suzie, I obsessed about it. I was up nights wondering how to handle this problem. Before I make any decision, I have to digest the issue. I've got to be at peace with the decision. I realized that my only choice was to set an example by letting Suzie go. I knew it meant putting my Dropbox business in jeopardy. It was a double-edged sword, but I had to maintain credibility and respect with my team.

When I brought Suzie into my office and delivered my decision, she was not happy. I gave her a severance package, which she accepted. Still, she wasn't happy. Unbeknownst to me, she called Dropbox right away and told them she'd been let go. She got to them first.

When I called Dropbox to say Suzie was no longer with Acrobat, they already knew. I explained what happened and how I had a plan in place. I assured them someone else just as good would take her place. But they didn't like it; they wanted Suzie and demanded I bring her back. They were mad, but I held my ground. We went through some rough spots with Dropbox but, in the end, it all worked out.

I gave Suzie a great reference. Ultimately, she ended up working for my top competitor as a staffing manager. After a while, the dust settled at Acrobat. Our team was more cohesive than ever. Everyone respected the decision I made, and the Dropbox account flourished.

After winning San Francisco's Small Business of the Year award and successfully expanding Acrobat into so many new markets, I felt pretty good about the state of the business. It was in great shape. Our culture was solid. Our model was sound. And the business was dispersed evenly throughout all the offices – not one account was bringing in more than ten percent of my overall revenue. In the past, I always worried about having a high concentration on just one or two accounts. It makes a company vulnerable. Losing one big account (such as Apple) can devastate your business. I was determined never to let this situation happen again, and we accomplished that goal. I knew we were a viable company. That's when I started getting inquiries from larger companies interested in acquiring Acrobat.

I was sitting at my desk one day when one of these inquiries came in. The woman on the phone introduced herself as Betty and said she represented a large hospitality services company that was looking for acquisitions. Even though I had no intention of selling my business, I felt I owed it to myself to hear out these inquiries. Betty was a business broker, and the company she represented was one of the largest hospitality services companies in the nation. It wanted to acquire a hospitality temporary staffing agency to round out its portfolio. She asked if I'd meet with this company's executives. I had nothing to lose so, even though I told her my company wasn't for sale, I would take the meeting. This was the first time I actually agreed to meet with someone about acquiring Acrobat.

A few weeks later, several of the company's executives came to my office to discuss a potential acquisition. They introduced themselves as TSC, which provides services exclusively to the hospitality industry. Within just a few minutes of our conversation, I felt a connection. It turned out a few of their executives spent many years with Hyatt. In addition, the CEO went through the Hyatt corporate management training program at the same time I did, and we knew some of the same people. I liked these guys. After the meeting was over, they asked if I would be interested in taking another meeting in Las Vegas to meet their investors and other executives within the company. I agreed.

The meeting would involve TSC's entire executive committee including, most notably, the CFO. I was told the company's CFO would be a hard sell. He was not sold on acquiring a temporary staffing company, because TSC had been burned in the past on a previous acquisition. In addition, I was told to be prepared, because the chairman of the private equity group was a brilliant guy who would ask some pretty tough questions. I remember thinking that I had nothing to lose, because I wasn't selling my business anyway. If they didn't want to move forward, I would be at peace with that. Before the meeting, I put together a PowerPoint presentation on Acrobat Outsourcing. Then I flew to Las Vegas for the meeting.

Now it was show time. Although I wasn't interested in selling my business, I connected with this company. I really liked these guys. Our philosophies on business matched. It appeared this company had a lot of momentum, and I wanted to be part of it. I thought partnering with or getting acquired by TSC would open up huge opportunities for Acrobat and give us access to new customers. By the same token, we would be able to introduce them to some of our customers. It seemed like a perfect fit. So I gave that pitch everything I had.

Standing there, in front of the entire executive team and key investors, I shared my story, my vision, and ultimately my entire business. I stepped through the life cycle of my business. How I started the company, how I grew the company, how I faced adversity, and how I rebounded from it. I spoke with passion and enthusiasm. I remember watching their body language and seeing them buy into the business and my vision. I can honestly say that I knocked it out of the park.

After I was done with my presentation, they peppered me with questions. Their CFO started by asking about the financial state of my business and my one-year, three-year, and five-year forecasts. The chairman of the private equity group focused on my growth strategy, how we overcame losing the Apple account, and how we replaced that business. I answered all the questions with pure honesty and supported my answers with facts. As the meeting concluded, I could tell they liked what I had to say. I saw the buying signs. Then they said they were ready to take it to the next level. So I signed a letter of intent to start the deal-making process.

The next step was negotiating a deal we could both agree to. Since I'd never been acquired, I hired an experienced merger and acquisition "rock star" to help negotiate the deal. Vicki had a tremendous amount of experience negotiating deals. I knew she had my best interest at heart and would help me negotiate the best deal possible. She audited my books, looked at my business trends, and did a pro forma showing anticipated revenue for the next five years. We came up with a realistic EBITDA (earnings before interest, taxes, depreciation, and amortization) to determine what my business was worth. We shared that number with the CFO of TSC. The CFO did not agree with that number and was determined to start some hard negotiating. He and another member of the executive team came to San Francisco to meet with me and Vicki.

It was a tough meeting to sit through – the negotiation was hard and it became fairly contentious, because we couldn't agree on the numbers. We went back and forth for hours, inching closer and closer to a deal. Finally, after about eight hours of negotiating, we reached a tentative deal. I was at peace with it, and all that was left was putting together a term sheet, which would state the conditions of the agreement. The TSC executives flew back to their headquarters, while I waited for the formal term sheet.

The next day I carefully reviewed the term sheet. I noticed they excluded paying me for my accounts receivable (AR). This is business that I already paid for (by paying the temp employees' wages) and was waiting on customers to pay me for services rendered. It amounted to $1.5 million dollars, which in essence lowered the sale price by $1.5 million dollars. This was a deal breaker; AR had to be included in the deal. I called the CFO and explained that he needed to pay me the AR to get the deal done. But he pushed back and said they'd made their final offer. If that was the case, I said, then we didn't have a deal. I declined the offer.

The whole thing felt crazy, because I'd just walked away from a multimillion-dollar offer, and who knew if another offer would ever come along. I was a bit distraught, but I knew in my heart of hearts that I was making the right decision. For Acrobat, it would be business as usual moving forward. Although I was willing to sell my business for the right price, I was not willing to discount my price just because I liked these folks. At the time, I didn't tell anyone at my company that I'd gotten so close to selling my business.

The following Monday – after I'd spent the entire weekend lamenting that I'd walked away from the deal – the CFO called and asked me to reconsider. But my mind was made up. I was determined to continue growing my business, and I was confident that, when the time was right, another deal would come my way. I politely told him I wasn't interested right now but maybe our paths would cross again. He was cordial, but he wasn't very happy.

I must've fielded ten or fifteen calls from private equity companies and other potential buyers after I declined the offer from TSC. Although things didn't work out with TSC, I could see that I must be doing something right if investors were coming out of the woodwork.

Instead of selling my company, I started looking for acquisitions and continued to focus on growing our existing business. Our business had been growing steadily; we had offices on the West Coast, in Texas, and in New Jersey. If I could open an office in the Midwest, then my business would really be nationwide. And that would make my company more valuable if I had another chance to sell it.

When I started looking around, I found a company for sale based in Kansas City, Missouri, which had a second office in Des Moines, Iowa. I went to Kansas City and vetted the company. It was much bigger than the company I'd acquired in Los Angeles, but I assumed everything would transition just as smoothly. I moved forward with the acquisition, went through due diligence, and looked "under the hood" as much as possible. Everything seemed to look good, so I purchased this company for about $750,000. This immediately brought in $7 million of revenue for Acrobat, and it gave us exposure in the Midwest, where we could take advantage of some of our established vendor agreements. Shortly after I bought this company, I started finding a lot of so-called skeletons in the closet.

The biggest problem was that most of their temp employees were not E-verified, which meant they didn't have the legal papers to work in the United States. This was a huge challenge because, at Acrobat, we had to make sure everyone was eligible to work. All temp employees needed to provide a Social Security number, be E-verified, and pass a background check. When I started looking at the files for these temp employees, I discovered that over half of them were not legal.

The other challenge with the acquisition was that I had to agree to bring on the owners. It was run by two brothers and a sister, and I agreed to bring them into Acrobat as employees. However, I quickly realized that our cultures didn't mix. We had very different styles of management. The previous owners didn't share information with their internal employees, so the staff members had no idea how much revenue they were bringing in and they didn't know their pay rates and bill rates. All the systems were out of date, and everyone was essentially doing their own thing. Records were kept by hand, so we had to transfer everything into the systems Acrobat used to keep the business organized. It was like the wild, wild West.

Then, as we were going through the entire process to vet the temp employees and clarify the actual numbers, we found out that one of the supervisors was stealing from the business. She was collecting her salary, and she had inserted herself into the books as an employee in a hotel, so she was also getting a weekly check as a temp employee. We uncovered this, because we were reviewing all the accounts and going through our rosters, and discovered there was an extra employee working as a housekeeper who didn't match the roster.

Unfortunately, we had to file a police report. The previous owners didn't want to press charges, because they were friends with this supervisor. But we were not friends, and I felt it was my civic duty to file a police report and have her arrested for stealing. We went to court, and she had to pay $17,000 back to Acrobat in restitution. But she didn't pay back the money that she had ripped off from the previous owners, because they didn't want to press charges. They just wanted her to go away.

We also had problems in the Des Moines office. The person in charge of that office, one of the previous owners, was not liked or respected by his fellow employees. People described him as reckless and unapproachable. He would fly off the handle and be disrespectful to employees. I had worked too hard to build a great culture within my company, and I had no tolerance for anyone who was mean or disrespectful. After many conversations with him, I knew he would never fit in the Acrobat culture.

So there were conflicts from the beginning – conflicts about my business philosophy and how to do things. The final straw happened when I found out a group of temp employees working as bartenders at a Kansas City football game never received their tips. A local TV station did an undercover investigation and a group of our employees went on camera to complain about not getting their money. One of the previous owners made a statement to the reporter on camera, denying any wrongdoing. I didn't even know this was happening until after the news story aired. My policy was that no one could talk to the press without me knowing, and we always handled delicate matters like this internally. When I found out they'd talked to the press, I felt betrayed. I questioned their loyalty to me and Acrobat.

After that, I decided to fire the two brothers and sister (the previous owners) who were running things in the Midwest. When I'd bought the company, I thought that magically the cultures could merge. But the way we managed our businesses couldn't have been farther apart. The offices could never be Acrobat offices under their oversight. After letting these three go and losing the supervisor who'd been stealing money, we were left with just a few internal employees and a handful of legal temp employees. To get Acrobat going in the Midwest, we had to break down that previous business and rebuild it.

Looking back, I didn't really know what I was doing. This company was three times the size of my other acquisition. I assumed the employees would be legal, so I never checked. Admittedly, I was more interested in my ego. I thought it would be strategic to have a truly nationwide company, and I didn't care what was under the hood to a certain degree. I just wanted the land grab and to get some locations in the Midwest.

But the good news is we had some business. Once we hired new people, implemented the Acrobat systems, and got the machine going, we had the Kansas City and Des Moines offices right where we wanted them. Everything started going well. Despite the headaches and heartaches, this acquisition paid off.

In the meantime, the machine also got moving in New Jersey and Austin, and business was really starting to flow. When you go into a new market, it takes a while to get everything working. By this point, all our offices were running smoothly and bringing in revenue. That's when I made the strategic decision to open a Houston location.

We didn't have any business in Houston, but I looked at it this way: What Silicon Valley is to software, what L.A. is to the entertainment business, and what New Jersey is to the pharmaceutical business, Houston is to the oil business. Houston had all the dynamics I looked for when I built out a new location. It had a lot of corporate business because of the oil industry. It had colleges and universities. It had professional sports teams. And it's the fourth largest city in the country.

So we put an employee in Houston to start staffing and another employee to start selling. Right out of the gate, we secured a big account, the Houston Zoo, and that got us going. This account catapulted us to new business and additional success thanks to our preferred vendor status with Sodexo and Aramark. Houston quickly became a viable market.

Although I walked away from millions that year from a potential acquisition by TSC, within one year, Acrobat grew from seven to eleven locations. Our revenue increased substantially. In fact, we were worth a lot more than what I'd been offered by TSC.

On-target business advice

Tips to build out your business to maximize the value

Most entrepreneurs I speak with ask, "How can I maximize the value of my business when it comes time to sell?" I've given this question a lot of thought, and I've come up with a formula that can pertain to most businesses. However, before I proceed, it's important to know that when it comes time to sell your business, you need to know how a buyer thinks.

Businesses are sold based on the seller's current and past EBITDA and how it's trending moving forward. EBITDA (earnings before interest, taxes, depreciation, and amortization) is the benchmark that's used to determine the value of your business. Usually a company with an annual EBITDA of $100,000 to $2 million can be sold for three to five times multiple EBITDA. For example, if your company is trending about $1 million in annual EBITDA, then you can assume that you can sell your company for a figure between $3 million to $5 million. If you can build your EBITDA to above $2 million, the multiple increases. Here are ways to maximize the value of your business.

Aim for a balanced customer concentration

You never want any one customer account to make up more than ten to fifteen percent of your overall revenue. This makes your company vulnerable if you happen to lose the big account, especially if it's a high concentration of your overall revenue (over twenty-five percent). It's very difficult to overcome a loss of that magnitude and stay the course to continue growing your business while replacing that revenue. Furthermore, if you were to lose that customer, it has a direct effect on other aspects of your business such as potential layoffs, cutting needed expenses, closing offices, and an overall negative effect on morale and culture. It's much easier to overcome the loss of a customer that makes up ten to fifteen percent of your overall business as opposed to a customer that makes up fifty percent.

Manage your expenses

I recommend you keep a close eye on expenses. Put a procedure in place to ensure you or one of your managers approves all expenses. Create an incentive program for your managers and/or employees to track expenses versus budget. This can be tied to your annual bonus plan. Pay a portion of bonus based on how much your team saves on expenses. For example, if you spend $500,000 annually for expenses and your budget is $600,000 then you just saved $100,000 annually in expenses. If you were to pay out $20,000 in bonuses, you've now saved $80,000 to your bottom line. This increases your profit by $80,000. In addition, you've just increased the value of your overall company by $80,000, and you've incentivized your employees to watch their spending.

Keep your vendors honest

Discipline yourself (or one of your employees) to get annual bids from your vendors for products or services rendered. It's amazing how many products or services needed to run your business are negotiable. Workers Compensation insurance and liability insurance are two large expenses that most companies need. You may notice that there are huge variances in insurance coverage and costs. Make sure you're comparing apples to apples when getting bids. You want to be properly covered, but you also want to lean on your vendors for the best quote and price. The bigger you get, the more leverage you'll have. The same goes with phone and high-speed Internet vendors, IT vendors, and all other service providers. Also, stay up to date on all of your vendors' promotions, rebate programs, and other vehicles to take advantage of additional savings. Negotiate, negotiate, negotiate.

Keep a close eye on travel and entertainment expenses

Most companies require some of their employees to travel for business. Be proactive to save on travel costs. Make airline, hotel, and rental car reservations in advance as often as possible. Last-minute travel can be expensive. Try to be as proactive as possible by booking early. You'll be delighted how much you'll save on your travel budget.

When it comes to business dinners, entertaining your customers, or teambuilding events, it's not necessary to go all out. You can accomplish a lot of business deals, cultivate relationships, and improve employee morale without overspending at top restaurants or entertaining clients on exclusive golf courses. Here's an idea: Instead of taking your clients to the best restaurant in town, take them to the fifth best restaurant in town. Instead of taking them to the most expensive golf course in town, take them to the second or third best course in town. You'll be amazed how much money you'll save and still be able to provide a memorable experience.

Create additional revenue streams into your business

One strategy that I find pretty powerful is the ability to add additional revenue streams into your business. The more revenue streams you have coming into your business, the less vulnerable you become if you lose a big customer or you're faced with an economic downturn or full-blown recession. Having multiple revenue streams is also very attractive to a prospective buyer. Take a macro look at your business to see if there are other ways to generate revenue. For example, one of my clients owns a pet grooming business and was looking for a way to expand. I suggested adding pet sitting as a revenue stream. This client was able to start generating new revenue from day one simply by using the existing customer database to announce and sell this new service.

Perception is reality – diligently manage your brand

I tell my clients all the time that you want your company to be perceived as bigger than it actually is. In order to do so, you need to be vigilant about managing your brand – your business name, logo, and reputation. You want to be regarded as a market leader in your industry. Protect your logo and brand. Make sure the product or service you provide is consistent. Try to exceed your customers' expectations. Be disciplined with all available marketing tools to be visible in your market. Utilize social media. Don't be controversial in your message and always be on point.

Market, market, and market your business

As the business owner, you are the face of your business. What you say or do with your business can be beneficial or detrimental. Your reputation is earned, and if you've earned a great reputation with your customers and your competitors, then you're on your way to success. Word of mouth sometimes can be your best resource to grow your business. It also can hurt your business. I tell my consulting clients that, as the business owner, you need to always be authentic, back up what you say, and deliver what you say. And remember, "The truth shall set you free." When selling your business, you want to make sure you have a sterling reputation with your customers and your employees.

Plan your exit strategy

You should start planning at least a year before you decide to sell your business. When it comes time to sell your business, you want to make sure all of your financials are up to date and your business is trending in the right direction. You want to make sure there is a strategy in place to overcome any economic downturn or recession. Also, make sure employee morale is high and your customers are happy with your product or service.

Don't let your ego stop you from selling your business

I find that most of my clients who are ready to sell their business get emotional about what they think their business is worth. Most owners think their business is worth more than what the market dictates. The truth is, your business is worth what someone is willing to pay for it. That's why you want to make sure you've positioned your company correctly for sale. Try not to get so emotional about your business that you price it too high (or too low). Objectivity is key. I recommend hiring a professional who has great business acumen to determine what a business is worth. A good business broker, merger-and-acquisition expert, or a business consultant (such as myself) can help you determine the right price.

Chapter 11

The post-sale rocky road

A year after I walked away from negotiations with TSC, the CFO called again. He said the chairman of the private equity company that owned TSC was coming to San Francisco and wanted to meet me for dinner. I had a feeling he was making a special trip, because TSC wanted to revisit the acquisition. I agreed to have dinner with him, and TSC made a reservation at Boulevard, one of the top restaurants in San Francisco. It's known as the place where power deals get done.

Dinner started with small talk and a bottle of wine. We talked about the state of TSC's business and the state of my business. Then the chairman of the board said, "Steve, I'm going to cut to the chase. We're still very interested in acquiring Acrobat Outsourcing."

"You know," I said, "I'm open to it, but negotiations broke down, because you weren't going to buy my AR, which was $1.5 million."

The chairman said, on the spot, "Well, we've had a change of heart. We'll include the AR."

I explained how my company was in a different state than it was when we were negotiating the last time. I had acquired another company with locations in Kansas City and Des Moines. In addition, I opened a couple of organic offices – Houston and San Bernardino – that I didn't have before. My company was worth more than it was a year ago. If TSC wanted to restart the negotiation process, we'd have to start from scratch. He agreed. After dinner, we wrote a Letter of Agreement and entered due diligence.

One reason I liked the idea of selling Acrobat was to mitigate my risk – both financially and from a liability standpoint. I didn't want to continuously worry about one of my temps getting into trouble, because some people just don't think before they act. This thought used to keep me up at night, and I wanted to get this liability off my back. I also saw radical changes in the staffing business that impacted my financials. It was becoming more difficult to do business in the city of San Francisco due to new regulations and employment laws. When you own your own business, you fight for your business 24/7. You worry about your business all the time. I didn't want to do that anymore. Plus, we were doing so well, I knew I'd be able to get a nice value for Acrobat.

For the next six weeks, a team of auditors and consultants dug into my business. They scoured the financials, performance, and trends to verify everything

I'd told them. This process was stressful. I had nothing to hide, but it felt violating to have people digging around in my business. I tried to look at it as a learning experience. I'd been through acquisitions before, but nothing this extensive. I bought one company for $250,000 and another for $750,000. TSC was willing to buy my company for eight figures. They wanted to take a good look under the hood, and they spent weeks scrutinizing my financials and business models. I realized I was in over my head, so I brought in the same merger-and-acquisition specialist to work hand-in-hand with TSC's investors and analysts.

The acquisition process was also stressful, because I didn't want to tell my employees why these strangers were coming into the office. When people asked, I told them the bank was auditing us. I hated being dishonest, but I didn't want anyone to get nervous.

As we were going through due diligence, I added a few more must-have requirements into the deal. The number-one requirement was to work as a separate entity under TSC's umbrella. I didn't want anyone coming into Acrobat, dismantling the business, changing the name, or changing the targets we were going after. I wanted to manage my business the way I managed it from day one. We had created a great culture, the business was thriving, morale was high, and we were growing. I didn't want to disrupt that momentum.

In the meantime, I was getting calls from other private equity groups asking if I was interested in selling Acrobat. However, because I was so far down the road with TSC, I put these inquiries on the sidelines until the due diligence process with TSC was done. But I knew I could use these inquiries as leverage on the sale price if I needed it.

When we were close to reaching an agreement, the unthinkable happened. One of my temp employees at the Des Moines office was killed on the job. In addition to staffing foodservice business, this office supplied temps for light industrial business. The accident took place in a tire factory. A tire fell off a machine, injuring this employee so severely that he died. Nothing like this had ever happened at Acrobat before, and I felt terrible. The employee was a single father, so I was really worried about his family. It was a devastating situation. From a business standpoint, I worried about whether our insurance would be able to settle with the family and whether this would impact negotiations with TSC. Acrobat paid for the funeral, and we did quite a lot for the family. Our team in Des Moines really stepped up. The insurance company settled with the family, and this unfortunate event didn't hinder negotiations with TSC.

After six weeks of due diligence, TSC agreed to all my contingencies, and we were ready to move forward. It was a warm spring day in San Francisco. I was sitting in the office with my merger-and-acquisition specialist, the CFO of TSC, and the TSC senior VP of sales. TSC presented a number. At first, we didn't agree. My advisor and I thought Acrobat was worth more. We negotiated for an hour, and TSC got a little contentious. But I could tell they had been instructed to get the deal done. We agreed TSC would pay me eight figures for the company: fifty percent as cash up front, twenty-five percent in stock, and twenty-five percent in earn-out. I agreed to stay with the company for a minimum of three years. Once we all agreed to those contingencies, it looked like we had a deal.

Next, we had to go through due diligence with the attorneys; they spent four weeks reviewing every detail of the contract. Plus, we negotiated an employment contract for me. (Although I agreed to stay for three years, I needed to protect myself with a severance package if anything changed.) As with most negotiations, there were some disagreements between my counsel and their counsel. But at the end of the day, the contract was ready.

We had struck a verbal agreement on a spring day and, now, on July 30 we signed the contract. The deal was done. It just so happened that when the money hit my account, I was in Las Vegas with the TSC folks. We were discussing forecasts, but what better place to celebrate? Two of my top managers – my VP of sales and my director of operations – were with me. We went out to dinner, I bought bottles of wine, and we went bar hopping. I tipped like I was giving away Monopoly money! I may have gone overboard, but I had never had money like that. I grew up in a working-class family. For the first time in my life, I didn't have to worry about money. I had a nest egg for my wife and family, my kids' college tuition would be paid, and retirement worries were over. Everything was good.

When I got back to the office, I had to take care of something I was not looking forward to: I had to tell my employees we'd been acquired. That was stressful, because some of these people had been with me from the start. Now I had to tell them in a way that wouldn't make them nervous and start looking for another job. They'd all been so loyal to me and honest with me. This wasn't going to be easy.

At our August staff meeting, I told everyone I had an important announcement to make. I told them a company had approached me, because it was impressed with our business model and interested in acquiring Acrobat. I told them that, before I would even listen to offers, I had to make sure nothing would change for my employees except the signature on their paychecks.

I said, "I got into a conversation with these folks and told them what I was looking for regarding taking care of my employees. They agreed, and these concessions were actually put into the contract. So I'm here to tell you that nothing is going to change. Also, this company has deep pockets. They'll help us grow the business even more. This is going to be a good thing for everyone at Acrobat."

I had been so worried that I'd get backlash after I made this gut-wrenching announcement, but they understood. My team was behind it. But I was asked over and over again, "Are you sure nothing's going to change?" I assured them it would be business as usual at Acrobat.

And it was business as usual – for my employees. But I was dealing with a new company. It was a hard transition, because I was used to calling the shots. I was used to making the decisions. Acrobat was an extension of me – my personality was woven throughout the company. And my vision to create a leading, nationwide temporary staffing company brought us to where we were today. Now I had to work side-by-side with another company, and I saw immediately that our cultures were very different.

TSC didn't operate with the same level of teamwork. Phone calls and emails weren't returned quickly. I started getting frustrated. I liked these guys, but I didn't respect the way they conducted business. I had really worked hard to build a culture within Acrobat where employees and customers are *both* the customers. Employees and customers should be treated with respect. Phone calls and emails should be returned within twenty-four hours. It was frustrating when that didn't happen with TSC. I remember thinking: Be careful what you wish for. I had asked TSC to leave us alone and, boy, did they leave us alone.

I was promised that we'd have a close relationship, working to grow each other's businesses. Acrobat would be able to tap into TSC's resources and customer list for additional business, and TSC would be able to tap into our customer list for additional business. I hardly ever heard from TSC in the beginning. The only person I talked with consistently was the CFO about our financial performance. I had to be at peace with the fact that, although I liked these guys personally, I didn't love the way they did business.

A few months after the acquisition, the CFO called and said they wanted to acquire a temporary staffing company in Dallas that I had identified as a potential acquisition. But, unbeknownst to me, they were already talking to this company, vetting it, and negotiating with the owner. They'd moved forward on this initiative with very little input from me, and I was taken aback. I'd been through several acquisitions, and I'd learned a lot about what to look for in a potential Acrobat addition. I'd learned which mistakes to avoid. The only negotiation experience TSC had with a staffing company was with me. I knew that if, in fact, they acquired the company in Dallas, they'd put it under the Acrobat umbrella, and I'd be responsible for managing it.

At the very last minute, they asked me to go to Dallas and take a look at the company. I saw a lot of red flags. In fact, it reminded me of the Kansas City situation – a lot of temp employees weren't legal to work in the U.S. Plus, the financials didn't make sense. But TSC was so far down the road in the negotiation process that my concerns had little effect on their final decision. They went ahead and purchased this company.

The acquisition included two locations: Dallas and Houston. Since we already had a Houston location, the plan was to combine that company's Houston business with Acrobat's Houston business. But Dallas was new territory. When the deal closed, I flew out and met everyone in both offices. I realized from the get-go that this would be a problematic acquisition.

The former owner was slick, and what he sold to TSC was a bag of rocks. He didn't tell us he'd just lost his biggest account, and he didn't revise the forecast. Most of the company's temporary employees – and internal employees – were not eligible to work in the U.S. The manager in the Houston office ran the place like a dictatorship. Her management style was intimidating. There was also division in the company. The Dallas office had six internal employees. Three sat on one side of the room, three sat on the other, and they didn't speak to each other! There was no teamwork. Instead, there was backstabbing, dysfunction, and insubordination. We had a mess on our hands, and we had to figure out how to build that business and make our numbers.

I made the difficult decision, like I did in Kansas City, to break it up and rebuild it. We let go of the senior staffing manager in Houston – the dictator – because we couldn't tolerate that kind of behavior. We kept the other Houston employees and had them work in tandem with our existing Houston office. With these changes, we were able to really grow that Houston business.

However, Dallas was more challenging. We let go of two of the office employees who were not eligible to work in the U.S. Plus, I let go of the drama king-pin who kept everyone working against each other. I brought people in from Austin and some of my other offices to help with that transition. Next, we audited the temporary employees. Most were not eligible to work in the U.S. We had to implement some major recruiting efforts to build up the roster. During this transition, we lost about half of the business.

I tried to explain these challenges to TSC, but they didn't understand. The executives were nervous, because this new acquisition was losing revenue. They pressured me to get the numbers back up. It took a lot of work and, after about six months, we did it. The Dallas-Houston business started growing.

I also learned that TSC's pockets weren't as deep as I'd thought they were. TSC was looking at another ac-quisition, a temporary staffing company in Phoenix. This time, TSC involved me from the start. I went to Arizona with the senior management team, met with the owners, went through due diligence, signed non-disclosure agreements, and signed a letter of intent. I was excited about this company. It was similar to Acrobat. The company had a lot of great accounts, and no account made up more than ten percent of the overall book of business. And most of the temp em-ployees were legal. We were really excited about bring-ing this Phoenix company on board.

But the private equity company that owned TSC, unbeknownst to me, was running out of money. At the eleventh hour, we had to walk away from this acquisition, because we couldn't afford it. This was embarrassing. After weeks of going back and forth in the negotiation process, the owners thought their company was about to be acquired. But we left them at the altar. That's when I started thinking TSC wasn't everything it seemed to be. The Dallas-Houston acquisition had left a bad taste in my mouth, and now we were walking away from the Phoenix deal. Although quarter after quarter, Acrobat was making our numbers and growing, I was sitting through TSC board meetings and seeing that the company as a whole wasn't making its numbers. In fact, TSC was losing business.

At one point, I went to the CEO of TSC and asked if I could buy back my company. He told me, adamantly, no.

By this time, the economy had gotten hot. Unemployment rates were dropping lower and lower, which meant recruiting employees to work on a temporary basis was getting harder and harder. The power shifted to our temp employees. They could ask for a higher hourly rate, because they had other opportunities. Often, we were pushed into a corner and needed the workers, so we'd have to give them the higher wage. We couldn't pass the higher cost on to our customers, because we had contracts with them. Our profit margins started shrinking.

In addition, one of our largest customers, Sodexo, put out a request for proposal to get bids for its preferred temp staffing vendor. Since our margins were higher, our proposal wasn't as attractive as some of our competitors' proposals. Sodexo asked us to lower our bid, but I made the strategic decision not to change it. We'd be spinning our wheels and working for very little profit. Sodexo decided to go with several smaller companies that were willing to accept a lower profit margin. We lost the preferred vendor status, and we lost a tremendous amount of business.

I was nervous, but I knew I had to hold my ground. I couldn't agree to Sodexo's terms, because we wouldn't make money. My key Acrobat employees, especially my VP of sales, were nervous too. I knew in my gut that Sodexo would be back, and I told everyone to be patient. Sure enough, three months later, Sodexo called and said that some of the companies couldn't fill their orders. They wanted to reinstate Acrobat in California, and we used that as leverage to get all Sodexo business back.

Those were a tough three months. But when it comes to your business, you have to believe in what you do, the value you provide, and your price. I wasn't going to let my business become a commodity. I didn't want to be the lowest-priced provider.

Sodexo also brought about a change in our pricing model to compensate for the increase in temp employee pay. We had always charged our customers a markup on the bill rate. Now we charged a markup on the pay rate. This was completely different from the industry standard; I think we were the first hospitality and foodservice staffing company to come up with this business model. Our customers agreed to the new structure, because they needed the temp employees. This new pricing model improved our bottom line dramatically, and it got TSC off my back. Plus, it protected the temp employees, because I could pay them more. This was a revolutionary change for Acrobat. Once again, we were making money, growing our business, and growing our profit margin.

Acrobat went into the second year with TSC with business growing. We got our hands around the pricing model, had two new locations, and were firing on all cylinders.

That year, TSC decided to make another acquisition, this time in Atlanta. With my involvement, to some degree, TSC bought the largest foodservice temporary staffing company in the city. This transition was much easier than the Dallas-Houston acquisition, because the Atlanta business had been run pretty well.

But as soon as we acquired the Atlanta company, the owner started spending a lot of money. Instead of keeping it lean and mean he moved the office to a much more expensive location. He signed a ten-year lease, which is unheard of in our industry. He bought new furniture and spent a ton of money. Technically, the owner reported to me. Since this acquisition wasn't fully under the Acrobat umbrella, I hadn't been keeping a very close eye on him. When the profit margins started shrinking, TSC asked me to get more involved. TSC executives wanted the Atlanta location to be fully incorporated into Acrobat to take advantage of our reputation and our preferred vendor status.

It's hard for one business owner to manage another business owner. Unbeknownst to me, he went over my head to the CEO of TSC and pitched the idea of opening a new location in Orlando, Florida. The CEO agreed with him. They started pumping a lot of money into this new office, but they couldn't get it off the ground.

In the meantime, the private equity company that owned TSC and Acrobat started having more financial issues. The investors couldn't afford to open new locations without seeing immediate revenue. They told TSC to close Orlando, because they couldn't afford to finance it.

The previous owner shut down Orlando and left the company. I went to Atlanta to fully bring the Acrobat culture to the office. The Atlanta location was run by men, and you could sense a "boys' club" feeling as soon as you walked into the office. I couldn't have that. All my other locations were diversified with an equal number of men and women. So I promoted some of the women in that office and brought in some employees from our other Acrobat locations. This time, we didn't need to take the drastic step of breaking down the company and rebuilding it. I chose a different strategy. We worked hand-in-hand with our customers to ensure that, although we needed to replace some temp employees who weren't eligible to work in the United States, we immediately replaced

them with documented workers. We changed processes and procedures much more methodically. And we
did not lose any business in the process.

During the two years after Acrobat was acquired by
TSC, I learned an important business lesson. Although
I was happy Acrobat was acquired – and happy to
have a healthy nest egg – I learned that this stage of
the business journey isn't necessarily easy. Instead of
running my business the way I wanted to, I had to
deal with people above me making decisions. And I
may or may not agree with those decisions. I should
have expected this, but it was a surprise. And it took
some getting used to.

On-target business advice

How to conduct extensive due diligence prior to acquiring a company

As an entrepreneur, you're constantly on the lookout for new
business opportunities. Whether you want to buy a new business to kick off your entrepreneurial journey or expand your
existing business, acquisitions can be a rewarding yet cum-
bersome process. There is much work to do on the front end.
You need to first identify a company that's available for sale
and meets your budget. You want to find a company that you're
excited about, a company that plays to your strengths and,
most important, a company that you can grow and eventually

sell for much more than what you paid for it. Embarking on the journey of entrepreneurship is not without its risks. But as I've said throughout this book, I believe in "high risk, high reward."

Once you identify a business to acquire, that's when the real work begins. The first step is signing a nondisclosure agreement (NDA). This gives the seller protection, since you'll promise not to disclose confidential information about the company. Once the NDA is signed, the seller will disclose more about the business including limited financials, business operations, locations, name of the business, and so forth. You'll have a short period of time to go through all the information provided and come up with an initial offer price for that business. Once that offer is accepted, you now have about six weeks to conduct extensive due diligence. In this stage, the seller opens all aspects of his or her business for you to review. Keep in mind, your initial offer is nonbinding, which will allow you to revise your initial offer based on your findings during this extensive due diligence period.

Once the six-week due diligence period begins, you have your work cut out for you. You want to dissect every part of the business you're about to buy. You want to protect your potential investment, so it's extremely important to dive into every aspect of the business. Many of my clients get so caught up in the financials that they tend to overlook other aspects of the business. Based on my experience buying companies, it's extremely important to concentrate on all aspects of the business, not just the financials. Use the following checklist as a guide when you're considering acquiring a company.

Financials

Having a good financial picture of the company you're about to buy will give you a good idea of the financial health of that company. Here are items you want the seller to provide:

- Three to five years of financials and tax returns – You want to make sure the numbers the seller provides matches the tax returns. Look for discrepancies; if you see any, send a list of questions to the seller for clarification. You'll also be able to determine how the seller derived the asking price based on the EBITDA.

- Trailing twelve months of profit-and-loss statements – It's important to see and understand how the business is trending, and this will give you a snapshot of the company's financial stability.

- Revenue per customer – You want to make sure there is no heavy concentration on just one customer. You want to make sure the revenue is disbursed evenly (or close to it) per customer. You don't want just one or a handful of customers making up most of your revenue, because this makes the business vulnerable. My rule of thumb is to make sure that no one customer makes up more than twenty-five percent of your overall revenue.

- Margins and cost of goods sold (COGS) – You need to understand the profit margins and whether you'll have flexibility to increase your prices.

- Expenses – You need to see a list of expenses the company needs in order to run its business. Spend some time dissecting the expenses. You can determine, based on the list of expenses, where you can potentially cut to help increase your profit margins. You'll also be able to determine if additional expenses might be needed that were not disclosed – expenses that can have a direct impact on the P&L and can indicate whether you'll need to revise your initial offer.

- Budget – Most companies run off a budget. Ask to see if there is a budget in place to determine how the business is trending based on budget versus actuals. Is the budget realistic?

- Salaries and compensation plans – Ask for all salary information related to internal, temporary, contract, and any other employees needed to run the business. Look deep into the salaries to determine if every employee is needed or if there aren't enough employees to do the work. Try to determine if you're going to need to raise some employees' salaries due to seniority and tenure. A good rule of thumb is to increase the overall salary expense by ten percent, because you have to assume you'll need to give raises to your employees. This ten percent across-the-board salary increase may affect the purchase price.

- Insurance, Internet, IT provider, and all other service provider contracts – Check the costs and contract terms of all service providers. Make sure you won't be locked into any long-term contracts without the ability to get out. You don't want to be locked into any contract that expands over two years.

- Office lease – Ask for a copy of the office lease agreement. Make sure you can live with the terms. You want to ensure your lease is reasonable and isn't ready to expire. If so, renegotiate the lease terms with the landlord prior to buying the company, so you know what your costs will be as well as the length of term and the location of your business.

Sales

Take a close look at these sales-related documents:

- Sales pipeline – It's important to know what's on the sales forecast, so you can determine what future sales look like. You want to make sure the pipeline is full, so you can forecast growth for the company you're about to buy.

- Three-year customer list – It's important to spend some time on customer lists. You want to determine how long each customer has been buying from the company. Look for discrepancies on sales revenue. Here, you can determine if your top customers are still buying from you and what the potential is for other customers to increase their revenue and sales. If you notice that a top customer is no longer doing business with the company, you need to question this. It could have a direct impact on the final purchase price.

- Sales commission plan – Most companies compensate their sales folks with a commission plan. Make sure you agree with the commission plan and check to see if it needs to be revised. You want to make sure the sales employees are being paid fairly but, by the same token, you don't want it to be so rich that the sales team is making more money than your executives. If so, this can have a direct impact on the morale of the company.

- Sales revenue streams – You want to determine how the company makes money and what product or service is driving the revenue. Is there an opportunity to create a new revenue stream? If so, what would the initial investment be and how long would it take to get to profitability?

- Lost business – You need a Lost Business Report, so you can determine how much money you have lost due to customers no longer buying from the business. Is there a possibility of converting your lost business into recovered business?

Operations and culture

One of the most overlooked areas of due diligence during an acquisition is spending time understanding its operations. This is of the utmost importance, because it's the heart of the business. You want to spend time understanding the policies and procedures. What mechanisms are in place to ensure customers are happy and will continue to do business with the company? I recommend asking for a sample of the customer list; contact those customers to get a feel for what they think of the business. Call these customers directly and ask them to rate the company. Try to get them to talk about the company and get a feel for their overall satisfaction. It's amazing how much information you can get from customers.

Culture also falls under operations. It's critical to have a good feeling for the culture of a company before you buy it. Whether you're buying your first company or acquiring a company to integrate into your existing company, culture can make or break your acquisition success. It can be challenging to integrate two different cultures into one company. Also, trying to change a culture to match yours can be daunting. Spend time talking with the company's employees. You'll get a feel quickly if people like working for the company or not. You want to get a pulse on the company's morale. Spend time in the trenches and understand which employees are leaders and which don't bring much value. Make your own decisions about people. Whether an employee can fit into your culture is critical to the success of the company.

Other key considerations

It's also important to learn and understand all compliance issues related to this business. Ask for all business licenses and pending lawsuits (if any). Ask for any Workers' Compensation ex-MODs, since Workers' Comp injuries can affect rates. Ask for all customer contracts, agreements, and programs such as rebates or sheltered income programs that you would be obligated to uphold.

Collect all customer reviews and look for any positive or negative trends in service, reliability issues, or any other issues that will have a direct impact on your purchase decision. The more information you can obtain about the business, the better. The power of information will help you make a sound business decision about whether to move forward with buying the company.

Once you dissect all of the information about the business, you now have an opportunity to revise your purchase offer. You have one last opportunity to renegotiate the purchase price if you see fit. When you purchase a business, it's all about how much you pay for it. Remember, the ultimate goal is growing it to its fullest potential. The lower the purchase price, the more you can make when it comes time to sell.

This is just a snapshot of what to ask for when evaluating a business to buy. Remember, the power of having information – the ability to make a sound business decision – is key to buying a business. It's always a high risk when purchasing a business, but the reward can be well worth it. You need to extensively look under the hood, so you truly understand what you are buying.

Chapter 12

Time to go

As owner of Acrobat Outsourcing, I was used to calling all the shots and making all the big decisions. Eventually, I realized it was very hard for me to work for another company. I was no longer the leader who made the final decisions. I had to adapt to a culture that did not match my personal business philosophy. I had to go along with decisions, whether I agreed with them or not.

Getting acquired meant someone was so impressed with what I'd built that they were willing to pay me millions for it. But it meant relinquishing control. I had to come to terms with not being in charge anymore. Soon after TSC bought Acrobat, I knew the end was near for me. But I couldn't walk away. Not yet.

As I was struggling with my tenure at Acrobat, I found out the investors who owned TSC were ready to sell their investment. They wanted me to be part of the team presenting the TSC business model to potential investors and private equity groups interested in acquiring us. I had just gotten remarried and was back from my honeymoon. I was summoned to New York City with the rest of the TSC executives to meet with twelve potential investment groups. In this three-week process we would meet with up to three investment groups a day to present our business model. It would be a lot of work, but I was hoping that if we sold to a different investment group, it would change my mind about leaving.

When I arrived in New York, I was impressed with the list of potential buyers. Some of the largest private equity groups in the country would be in the room. We were meeting with well-respected companies with billions of dollars of credit as well as some smaller investment groups that focused on the hospitality industry.

The building we presented in is located on Park Avenue (location of the NFL headquarters). One by one, these companies' representatives came into the conference room and listened to our presentation. They asked precise and interesting questions. I was impressed with our executive team. We were all on our A-game, and we knocked each presentation out of the park. It also brought us closer together. After this process, I started to change my mind about leaving TSC.

After each day of presentations, we met at the hotel bar and recapped the meetings of the day. We were feeling good about ourselves. After three weeks of presenting, we left New York knowing we did our best and hoping we had convinced the investors to pay the highest multiple possible for the TSC family of companies. We waited for the next step – interested investors would need to make qualifying offers to gain access to our financials.

We'd done so well that every investment group signed a nondisclosure agreement to have full access to all financials and business models. This gave all investment groups access to TSC's current, past, and future financials, so they could dissect the numbers, come up with projections on current and future growth, and get to know the company they were considering buying. Usually after this process, a few companies leave and the ones left are considered serious buyers.

Unfortunately, the numbers were not impressive. While Acrobat was cranking on all cylinders – breaking revenue records and poised to grow thirty percent over the previous year – TSC's main business unit was bleeding cash. This unit was well below budget with no hope of recovery in sight. That business unit made up seventy percent of the overall revenue. The fact that it was losing money did not reflect well on the entire company. Many potential investors backed out of the deal. Only two companies of the original twelve wanted to move forward. This process allowed these two companies to revise their original offer. Since the financials were much weaker than expected, both companies revised their bids with a much lower offer. Both were low-ball offers.

One of these two companies was my least favorite. One of the executives came across as arrogant and condescending. He had a know-it-all attitude and was only interested in the bottom line. I was praying this company would not buy TSC.

If I'd had my way, I would've held off for another year, so TSC could grow its numbers and be poised for a higher value. I'd done this a few years earlier with Acrobat. By waiting just a year, I'd increased the value of Acrobat enormously. But TSC's investors were running out of money and needed to sell.

As luck would have it, the company I didn't want to work with purchased TSC. I knew it would be extremely difficult to work for this new private equity group. Worse, after the deal was completed, they named the guy I didn't like to be a top executive of TSC. At that moment, I knew my days at Acrobat were numbered.

When you buy a company, a rule of thumb is to spend the first sixty to ninety days just getting to know the company, the employees, and the industry. You don't make any drastic changes until you fully understand the nuances of the business and the direction you want to take it. It was clear from the outset that this guy was more interested in making a name for himself than doing what was best for the business. Literally, starting the first week on the new job, he initiated drastic changes that caused complete chaos throughout Acrobat – the company I built. He had no experience in the hospitality or foodservice industries. Even so, he thought he knew everything.

His first order of business completely tore apart Acrobat. He decided to fully integrate the Acrobat business into TSC (which was losing money) and do without the Acrobat name – the brand I had worked so hard to build! Next, he downsized the Acrobat accounting department (he laid off my entire accounting team) and integrated Acrobat into TSC's accounting department. But here's the problem: Acrobat was a separate business unit from TSC, and our accounting functions were very different. This meant TSC's accountants had to overcome a huge learning curve. He also wanted to scrap our proprietary software – the custom software program that keeps track of our entire business flow – and replace it with an off-the-shelf solution.

I pleaded with him, asking him not to move forward with these plans, since they would have a direct impact on the company's culture, morale, and bottom line. He didn't want to hear it. His decision was final. He said he did not want to hear another word about it. In the end, my team and I reluctantly supported his decision.

As the months passed, I realized the current company was much different from the one I spent fourteen years building. I grew my company into an industry-leading powerhouse with eighteen offices nationwide and $50 million in annual revenue. And now it was broken. Morale sank to an all-time low. Employees were paranoid about losing their jobs, and we started losing business. But my boss did not want to listen to anything I had to say.

I always promised myself that if I ever left Acrobat, I would leave on top. We had just finished the year with a thirty percent revenue growth over the previous year and almost $3 million EBITDA – double what it had been the year before. My team and I had worked hard to achieve, and surpass, every goal we set. But my hands were now tied. I was working for a man I didn't respect, and he was running my business into the ground. He was only interested in the short-term bottom line, with no appreciation for the business itself or the culture. I wanted to be a mentor to my employees and watch them grow and achieve, but that was no longer possible, because I had to support the direction of the company's new owners. The final decision was difficult to make, but the ride was over.

Chapter 13

Onward and upward: Sharing the entrepreneurial spirit

Never in a million years did I think I would be teaching entrepreneurship to college students. But the summer after I stepped down from Acrobat Outsourcing and started my consulting business, that's exactly what happened. I got an offer to teach summer school to incoming college freshmen at UC Berkeley. I found it so rewarding.

On my first day of teaching, I was nervous, because I didn't know exactly how to present what was inside my head. I've never taught before, so I didn't realize what I was getting myself into. But then again, I'm a firm believer in "high risk, high reward," and I knew that if I put in the work, the reward would be fulfilling. And that's exactly what happened.

That day, and over the course of the next few weeks, I talked to my students about bringing their ideas to life, making business plans, how to go to market, where to get funding, how to make it scalable, how to build a team, running day-to-day operations, making sure the business is resilient and resistant, and the importance of culture. The class was a high-level overview of all the different aspects of creating, running, growing, and ultimately selling a business.

During the semester, I packed as much wisdom into the class as I could, giving these young adults insight into the entrepreneurial life. I talked to them about how I built a company that would be scalable, then scaled it by going to different locations, and sold it for eight figures. I wanted to empower them with the knowledge of how to build something valuable that they could eventually sell, something that could fund their retirement.

In addition to providing tactical information and strategies they could use, I talked to my students about my personal business philosophy such as taking risks and social responsibility. I told them that, as entrepreneurs, they're responsible for growing and mentoring their people and setting them up for success. I urged them not to be afraid to think outside the box and take risks on people whom you normally would not hire such as military veterans, reformed ex-offenders, and people with special needs. When you're giving people jobs, you're contributing to their livelihood, and that's a powerful way to change someone's life.

My greatest pride is looking back on my years at Acrobat and knowing that the people who worked for me are better off today than they were when they first started. I taught them not to be afraid to take risks on people. As the business owner, you benefit too, because your people start growing into their positions and really building your business. But the fact that I was able to give them something they could carry with them – something they could use to flourish beyond the work they did for me – is what really inspires me. When you mentor people and help them grow, you become a part of their future success. That gift was given to me early in my career, and I owed it to myself to give it to the people who worked for me.

The teaching experience was a lot of fun. But, day after day, I could never really tell if I was getting through to my students. I was committed to teaching them what I learned throughout my career and hoped my experience, my philosophy, and my passion were getting through to them.

By far, my favorite part was the final project – they had to create a business plan and present it to me as if they were on *Shark Tank*. For this final project, the students formed small groups. And these students were from all over the world: Brazil, Lebanon, Romania, Russia, Spain, and the United States. Group by group, they presented their ideas to everyone in the class.

Let me tell you, these kids knocked it out of the park every time. For example, my group from Lebanon came up with the idea of bringing electric scooters to Beirut. The city had poor public transportation and massive amounts of traffic. Making electric scooters available would solve a critical community problem, which I thought was brilliant.

My group from Brazil/U.S. had a great idea they called "Instant Classroom" – they wanted to put vending machines with school supplies on high school and college campuses. If students needed a calculator or pen, they could go to these vending machines and get what they needed for class.

My group from Romania/Russia came up with a restaurant concept: flavors from around the world. They wanted to build the restaurant in four sections – north, south, east, and west – where different cuisines would be offered from the different quadrants of the world.

My group from Brazil came up with a beauty app that would allow people to order in-home manicure and pedicure services.

Watching these kids present their ideas, I knew I'd gotten through to them. Their business plans were remarkable and well thought out. They were thinking like entrepreneurs. It was so rewarding to watch students (who knew virtually nothing about business on the first day of class) as they developed the confidence, knowledge, and enthusiasm to embrace entrepreneurship as a career.

By the time the course was over, I knew I had gotten through to them. On the last day of school, every student came up to me individually and thanked me for teaching him or her about entrepreneurism. They all told me how inspired they were by my class. It was "high risk, high reward" at its finest.

I hope my story empowers you as well. Acrobat was my passion; Acrobat was my life. I was committed to my business. I had no choice but to make it work. And it was more challenging than I could ever have imagined it would be. But getting to share that experience and helping others on their business journey – whether you're a college student, seasoned business owner, or aspiring entrepreneur – has made it all worthwhile.

No matter where you are in your business journey, the most important thing you can do is bet on yourself. Take the risk. Go for it. And keep betting on yourself and your business. The rewards of doing so extend well beyond those of hard work and making a living.

On-target business advice

Checklist to prepare your exit strategy, so you can get the highest sale price possible

The most exciting part of your entrepreneurial journey is when you're ready to sell the company that you've poured your heart, sweat, and tears into. All the years that you've sacrificed so much of your time, money, and commitment to your business will be rewarded if you prepare your exit strategy correctly. Know that there is some prep work that needs to be accomplished before you actually list your business for sale but, if done correctly, you'll achieve the maximum value for your company.

The first thing to consider when it's time to sell is to make sure the economy is strong, and your business is healthy and growing. You want to have a track record of continued growth and a clear indication of sales momentum moving forward. It's best to sell your company when it has reached its potential and the year-to-year growth starts leveling off. Once that's in place, you're now ready to start the process to sell your business. I recommend starting this process about one year ahead of your listing. Here's a timeline of the preparation that needs to be done in order to receive the maximum value for your business.

Nine to twelve months before listing your business for sale

It's critical to have your financials in order before you begin your exit strategy. You want to go back at least three to five years to make sure your financials are in good shape. By the same token, make sure your tax returns match your financials. I can guarantee you that accurate financials are usually the first thing a buyer is going to request during due diligence. Unless you have a sharp finance team in place, I recommend hiring a CPA firm, highly experienced bookkeeper, or a merger-and-acquisition specialist to help you. I can help you as well. It's worth the upfront investment, because having your financials in order is one of the most important things you can do to prepare your exit strategy.

Once your financials are in order, it's now time to lock down your EBITDA (earnings before interest, taxes, depreciation, and amortization). The firm you hired to substantiate your financials can help you derive your EBITDA number, which is used to determine what your business is worth. Companies or individuals pay a multiple of your EBITDA to determine the final sale price. Your financial team will work with you to get an accurate EBITDA number.

If you haven't done so, you'll need to create an accurate budget and sales forecast. You'll need this moving forward to track your expenses and sales versus actuals. You want to show your prospective buyer that you're trending in the right direction and you have a good feel for your business. Providing this to your prospective buyer will show that you have your arms around the business.

I recommend drafting and sending a customer opinion survey to your customers. (You can find survey templates on the Internet or use an online survey tool.) You want to have a real feel for how your customers rate your company. It's important that your customers are satisfied with your product or service. Results from this survey also give you a heads-up about any issues you might need to fix. When it comes time to sell, you can provide your potential buyer with testimonials from your satisfied customers. This will give your potential buyer peace of mind.

This is also the time to analyze your expenses and see if you can cut any expenses to help improve your bottom line. It's in your best interest to have your P&L trending higher in the year you're ready to sell compared to previous years. You want to show business momentum.

This is also a good time to pressure your sales folks to fill the sales pipeline. You want to have a sales funnel that's full of opportunities with a high *probability* of converting to sales. In addition, you want to have other prospects on this list that show *potential* of converting to sales. Having this list will be beneficial to your buyer when it comes to closing potential business down the road.

Six to nine months before listing your business for sale

This is the time to concentrate on your marketing. You want your company to appear that it's larger than it really is. Make sure your website is up to date, and the content is relevant. Make sure you have a large online presence and you're utilizing the appropriate social media tools for your customers and your industry. Facebook, Instagram, LinkedIn, and Twitter are good resources to get your name out there. Monitor those sites and urge your customers and employees to "like" them. You want to show a prospective buyer that you have a large following.

This is also a great time to audit your operations. Make sure all of your policies and procedures are in place. You want to address any inconsistencies with your product or service at this time. This will allow you to focus on any issues and get them fixed, so your business can run as smoothly possible.

Spend time on your human resources practices. Review your employee handbook and make sure it's up to date. Audit all employee records and make sure all employees sign the handbook and non-compete clause. When it comes time to sell, it's critical that all of your employees are in employment compliance and have signed a non-compete form. Your buyer needs to have peace of mind that no one is going to try to duplicate your business or walk away with trade secrets.

Three to six months before listing your business for sale

Review all of your contracts. Make sure you aren't locked into any contract for more than two years. Any long-term contracts will be questioned by the buyer. This is now a good time to renegotiate any contracts that don't live up to expectations. You don't want your prospective buyer to be stuck with contracts that don't bring value to the business. Review your office lease. Make sure there is a minimum of one year left on your lease. Buyers can get spooked if the lease is about to expire once they buy the business. By the same token, you don't want to have too many years left on your lease, which can make your buyer feel locked in to that location.

Review your employee roster. Make sure all employees are up to date on employee performance evaluations. Make sure all salary increases are discussed and given if warranted. You don't want to have your buyer be responsible for salary increases at the time of purchase, because a savvy buyer will use the salary increases as a negotiating point to decrease the value of your business. (Salary increases have a direct impact on the bottom line.)

It's also important that employee morale is high because, when it comes time to sell your business, buyers are not simply buying your product or service – they are also buying your customer list, your phone number, and the goodwill of the employees who've helped to make your company successful.

Zero to three months before listing your business for sale

Put together a document that gives you a snapshot of your business. I suggest a handout that gives a prospective buyer a quick overview of your company. You can revise this as you get closer to the date you actually list your business, but it's a good teaser to give to your business broker or merger-and-acquisition specialist when it comes time to sell.

You're now almost ready to put your company up for sale. This is the time to determine how you want your company to be sold. Your specific exit strategy depends on the size of your company. If your EBITDA is less than $1 million, I suggest reaching out to a business broker to market and sell your company. Try to find the best business brokers in your area that specialize in your industry. Identify three to five top producers and interview them. Make sure you feel a connection with the broker. Also, it's important this person is in alignment with you on price, type of buyer you're looking for, and the structure of the deal.

If your company's EBITDA is higher than $1 million, I suggest hiring a merger-and-acquisition specialist to help you find your buyer. These folks work with private equity groups, venture capitalists, investment bankers, and strategic buyers. Once again, try to find three to five specialists you can interview. It's imperative that you have a great connection with this person, and he or she has your best interest in mind when representing you to sell your business.

A strategic buyer is a company that acquires other companies to fill a void in its array of products or services or to complement its current business offerings. It also could be a company that looks to buy competitors, so it can become a market leader in the industry. It's helpful to put together a list of companies that are similar to yours that you can approach for acquisition. Give that list to your broker/specialist, so he or she can reach out and see if there is any interest.

You need to be very involved in every part of the sales process. Stay in close contact with your broker/specialist and pressure him or her to find qualified buyers that can put forth an acceptable offer. The goal, of course, is getting the highest sale price possible.

About the author: Steve Scher

Small Business Advisor | Speaker

Steve Scher is a business advisor for entrepreneurs, small business owners, franchise owners, and aspiring entrepreneurs. As a business mentor, professional speaker, and acclaimed author of *High Risk, High Reward*, Steve guides business owners to achieve ultimate success and financial freedom. In particular, he's passionate about sharing proven strategies to:

- Build out your business to its full potential and maximum value.

- Strategically hire military veterans, reformed ex-offenders, and people with special needs.

- Conduct thorough due diligence to
  make an educated decision on whether
  to purchase a company.

An exceptionally successful entrepreneur, Steve previously served as CEO & Owner of Acrobat Outsourcing. Thinking he was buying a "diamond in the rough," it turned out this tiny, under-performing staffing company offered two unreliable employees and no real systems for sales, marketing, or operations.

During his fourteen years as CEO, Steve worked hard to overcome many business challenges and the many curveballs entrepreneurs experience throughout their careers, including economic downturns. In the process, he honed his leadership skills, learned the true value of employees, and understood the importance of creating a great culture.

Over the years, Steve forged his business into a leading temporary staffing company with eighteen offices nationwide, hundreds of loyal employees, and $50 million in annual revenue. This temporary staffing solutions company specializes in hospitality, foodservice, convention, and related industries. The impressive customer list includes Apple, DropBox, Fairmont, Google, Hyatt, and Marriott; elite university systems such as Stanford, UC Berkeley, UCLA, USC, and University of Texas; large hospital systems throughout the U.S.; and concessionaires for major league sports teams and events including multiple Super Bowls and World Series.

Over the years, Steve built a team and processes that could be scaled and replicated. While establishing coast-to-coast locations, he applied various strategies to build out the business. Eventually, he mastered a proprietary approach that delivers the best ROI in terms of efficiency, loyal employees, unified culture, and long-term profitability.

In the early years of running Acrobat Outsourcing, Steve personally interviewed and hired employees to fulfill organizations' temporary and permanent job openings. At last count, his company hired in excess of 100,000 employees to staff tens of thousands of jobs. Consequently, he gained extraordinary insight into recruiting and hiring high-potential employees.

In the process, Steve uncovered a "hidden" source of talent: military veterans, reformed ex-offenders, and people with special needs. Passionate about giving people a second chance, Steve guides business owners to give these people a second chance by applying a strategic approach, taking a calculated risk, and leveraging win/win results within their community and industry.

Eventually, Steve fulfilled the American dream of not just building a great business but also selling his business at maximum value.

In addition to consulting with small business owners, Steve teaches courses in entrepreneurialism at the University of California, Berkeley. He holds an AS degree in hotel and restaurant management and a BS degree in hospitality management. Steve's company was recognized as Small Business of the Year by the City and County of San Francisco in 2012 and is the recipient of multiple other awards and recognitions including Employer of the Year from JobTrain.

Steve enjoys spending time with his wife Elizabeth and their five kids. An avid sports fan, he often coaches kids' baseball and basketball teams. In his spare time, he loves to exercise, attend sporting events, and travel the world. Steve's life motto is: "Make every experience you have with someone a positive experience."

How can you maximize the value of your business?

Contact Steve Scher to start the conversation.
Steve Scher
Chief Executive Officer
Small Business Advisor | Speaker
Acrobat Advisors, LLC
Steve@AcrobatAdvisors.com
www.AcrobatAdvisors.com

CPSIA information can be obtained
at www.ICGtesting.com
Printed in the USA
FSHW022009041119
63767FS